CAREERS IN PLUMBING, HEATING, AND COOLING

CAREERS IN PLUMBING, HEATING, AND COOLING

By
ELIZABETH STEWART LYTLE

The Rosen Publishing Group, Inc.
NEW YORK

Published in 1995 by The Rosen Publishing Group, Inc.
29 East 21st Street, New York, NY 10010

First Edition

Manufactured in the United States of America

Library of Congress Cataloging-in-Publication Data

Lytle, Elizabeth Stewart.
    Careers in plumbing, heating, and cooling / by Elizabeth Stewart Lytle.—1st ed.
      p.   cm.
      Includes bibliographical references and index.
      ISBN 0-8239-2052-6
    1. Plumbing—Vocational guidance—Juvenile literature. 2. Heating—Vocational guidance—Juvenile literature. 3. Air conditioning—Vocational guidance—Juvenile literature. [1. Plumbing—Vocational guidance. 2. Heating—Vocational guidance. 3. Air conditioning—Vocational guidance. 4. Vocational guidance.]
    I. Title.
TH6130.L96 1994
696'.1'023—dc20
                              94-13577
                                CIP
                                AC

For my parents, Ed and Kathy Stewart, in Tucson, who have proved equal to the task of explaining how their daughter happened to write a book about plumbing

About the Author

Elizabeth Stewart Lytle is a photojournalist, teacher, and communications consultant in western Pennsylvania. She shares an interest in the construction trades and housing issues with her husband, a building contractor.

As a free-lance magazine writer, she focuses on home design and improvement topics, along with travel articles. She has more than 350 magazine article sales to her credit. As a contributing editor to *Your Home* and *Indoors & Out* magazines, her byline appears regularly in those pages. She has also written a number of career monographs and consumer articles for educational publishers in Chicago.

In pursuit of travel adventure stories, she has tried her hand at flying a soaring plane and has twice sailed the Saguenay River Fjord region of Quebec Province, Canada, to observe and photograph the summer migration of whales.

Mrs. Lytle has received several writing awards as a newspaper journalist and as a free-lance magazine writer. She also served three terms as a state director of the Pennsylvania Women's Press Association.

She has done considerable work in the Writer's Workshop at the University of Iowa, where she earned a degree in liberal studies and is a member of Alpha Sigma Lambda national honorary society. She is currently working on a master's degree in communications.

In 1991 the Franklin Area School District nominated Mrs. Lytle for the Sallie Mae First-Year Teacher Award, a program recognizing one hundred of the nation's outstanding new educators.

She and her husband are parents of one son, Christian.

Acknowledgments

This book would not have been possible without the support and encouragement of many people and organizations interested in the career field. The author wishes to acknowledge the help of Chet Lytle, for technical support; Maura Russell and Christine Ernst, master plumbers, of Boston; Nancy Falter, of the NAPHCC Educational Foundation; Henry Heid, UA Apprenticeship Director, Pittsburgh; the National Association of Home Builders and the Home Builders' Institute; the Pennsylvania College of Technology; the Job Corps; Lennox, Carrier, Kohler, and Malco Products Corporations; the U.S. Department of Labor and its Women's Bureau; and the U.S. Department of Energy.

Special thanks go to Betty Brinkerhoff for editing expertise and to Gina Strazzabosco, who guided the publishing process.

Contents

1

Welcome to the Industry

The work of creating and maintaining safe and comfortable indoor environments has grown into a rewarding career field for people with mechanical skills, particularly those who can operate sophisticated equipment. But what, you ask, is an indoor environment? Simply the systems that make a structure habitable and comfortable for human use. Regardless of the size of the building—from single-family home to 500-unit apartment complex, corner store, or enormous shopping mall—each has the same basic need for heating, cooling, water, and piping systems.

Likewise, in thousands of cities and towns across America, more than a million people have secure, rewarding careers in the plumbing, heating, ventilating, and air conditioning industries, which are commonly referred to as Plumbing/HVAC. Some work in the construction industry, helping to build new structures or renovating existing buildings. Others design, manufacture, sell, and install fixtures and equipment. Still others are hired to operate, maintain, and repair indoor environmental systems.

This work does not occur in a vacuum. Changes in society bring changes to the industry. The government and the citizens, too, are paying increasing attention to the need to conserve valuable natural resources. We have learned the importance of using less water and fuel. Industries concerned with indoor environments have accepted their responsibility to provide new, energy-efficient products, which in turn requires that their employees be flexible and willing to adapt to change.

BEGINNINGS OF THE INDUSTRY

Many of us tend to take the indoor environment for granted, yet the era of indoor plumbing and central heating is little more than a century old in many parts of the country. Climate control in the form of air-conditioning is even more recent. For example, in 1967 fewer than one in five homes and apartments in the United States had air-conditioning. This book is about career opportunities in several interrelated fields—plumbing, heating, ventilation, air-conditioning, and sheet-metal work. Career opportunities are also reviewed in another relatively new industry, refrigeration, which makes it possible to transport and store perishable products, including foods and medicines.

Workers who can install, operate, and repair elements of these indoor environmental systems are in demand. And the demand is sure to grow, since such systems are becoming increasingly sophisticated in both mechanical and electronic design. Also, as our standard of living continues to rise, there will be greater consumer demand for these systems in all parts of the nation, not just in regions of extreme climate.

LEARNING A TRADE

Career opportunities exist at various levels for beginning and experienced workers, depending on their training, adaptability, and willingness to learn. There are likewise many opportunities to learn the skills needed to succeed in the industry. Some are free of charge, others require tuition payments. Still others pay *you* to learn a trade, with wages that increase as your skill and experience grow. Perhaps best of all, the training period is far less than it takes to graduate from college.

You can begin learning these trades in high school vocational-technical programs and continue in trade schools and community colleges, the military services, and in the formal apprenticeship programs of labor unions and the industry.

If you left high school without a diploma, don't worry. The U.S. Job Corps will help you graduate and supply real-world job training at the same time.

Choosing to work in plumbing, heating, or cooling/refrigeration can mean job security, challenge, and rewards, both financial and personal. Once you are trained and begin to work, you will discover opportunities to advance to a position of real responsibility. For many people, variety is an important factor in choosing a career. They do not want to be stuck in the same place, performing the same repetitive task hour after hour. You will find much variety in all of these fields. You will travel from job to job, perform a variety of tasks, and keep up-to-date as the industry advances.

There will also be opportunities to move to a new, yet related field of endeavor, should you choose to. Often, the skills required in one segment of the industry are interchangeable with those of another, permitting workers to transfer from serving heating systems to air-conditioning installation or repair, with little time spent in retraining. Talented persons who begin in an entry-level stage of a career can, with experience, move into other professions—sales, job estimating, drafting, design, writing specifications, or working as a field or lab technician. Others may use the experience they gain to launch their own business.

Workers in this industry perform a variety of tasks, some of them readily visible, others hidden from view.

Even when the people occupying the buildings cannot see this labor, the trained professionals who performed the work have the satisfaction of a job well done. They know, too, that their work helps to raise the standard of living in communities across the country.

ORGANIZATION OF THE BOOK

This book is designed to introduce young people to those specific blue-collar trades related to indoor environments. We shall look at career possibilities in the fields of plumbing, heating, ventilating, air-conditioning, and sheet-metal working. A related field, refrigeration, is also included.

These industries are related in several ways and often overlap. For instance, in many parts of the country cross-training results in workers who are skilled at both plumbing and heating trades. In other geographic regions, you may find heating and air-conditioning mechanics who do little or no plumbing. Still other locales turn out HVAC mechanics, who specialize in heating, ventilating, and air-conditioning work. Businesses that service environmental systems generally employ sheet-metal workers, as do firms specializing in construction work. Air-conditioning mechanics may also handle refrigeration duties.

Regardless of differences in training and specific mechanical talents, all are involved in creating and maintaining indoor environments. We shall look at the education and training required of each. Chapter 13, "Vignettes," is a collection of interviews depicting the experiences of several real people who earn their living in these trades. You will learn firsthand how they go about creating, operating, or maintaining environmental environments.

Since much of your career will deal with the 21st century, we shall also look at the latest developments in solar energy, electronics, and other areas that will affect the way you will work.

Other chapters provide practical advice about seeking your first job, starting a business of your own, and discovering whether your talents and abilities are well suited to the demands that would be made upon you if you entered one of these careers.

Are these jobs in demand? Yes, indeed. The construction industry relies heavily upon young workers to fill vacancies. By the year 2000, as many as 70,000 jobs will be available to trained plumbers and pipefitters in the residential construction industry alone.

At the present time, about 250,000 workers are employed as heating, air-conditioning, and refrigeration mechanics. The U.S. Department of Labor predicts a 17 percent expansion in the number of these jobs, or 38,000 in the decade ahead. Along with new construction, the installation of residential climate control systems in existing homes is becoming more common. Such systems require regular routine maintenance, which should also create job opportunities.

As for sheet-metal workers, about 97,000 jobs existed in the construction industry at the close of the 1980s. Three of every four sheet-metal workers worked for a contracting firm, generally in plumbing, heating, and air-conditioning fields. Few workers in this category are self-employed. Employment in construction is expected to keep pace with increases in all occupations, though demand will be heaviest in construction.

How can you tell if a job in plumbing, heating, or cooling is for you? First, consider your own skills and aptitudes. These workers are known for their manual dexterity. Do you like to use tools? Are you interested in how things work? Do you have a basic understanding of mathematics, physical science, or physics? You should note that these jobs require physical stamina and a certain degree of strength to handle tools and materials. You must also be capable of reading and following blueprints, schematics, or verbal instructions. Most of all, however, these trades require the ability to plan and solve problems.

Interested? Then read on. A practical and rewarding career awaits you.

2

An Overview of Occupations

As a trained technical worker in plumbing, heating, ventilation, air-conditioning/refrigeration, you use your hands and your head to create and maintain necessary structural systems. You may work alone or be part of a team. You may work indoors or out. You may travel or spend your time in a shop or an office; you may be part of a corporation or a small business, or manage your own business. There are opportunities to increase your knowledge and skill and advance to supervisory, administrative, or engineering positions in private industry, education, or government. You may also choose to launch your own service or contracting business in one of these trades.

Whether you prefer to live and work in an urban area or a rural setting, you should be able to find opportunities anywhere in the United States. Like adventure? There are career opportunities at sea and in many foreign countries. Few industries offer such diversity in places of work. Because the skills and knowledge required in these trades overlap, it is also possible to move from one field to another with minimal retraining.

In addition to jobs in the building trades and the installation and service industries, you can consider a number of manufacturing and sales support careers within a vital and growing industry. For example,

Lennox Industries, Inc., an internationally recognized leader in building high-efficiency heating and air-conditioning products, operates 46 distribution centers and 33 district sales offices, with more than 225 territory managers on staff. Workers at each of these facilities must understand both the heating and cooling industry and the company's products. More about related opportunities in a moment. First let's take a closer look at the plumbing/HVAC trades themselves.

PLUMBING

Plumbers are in demand in the construction and renovation of homes and buildings, in addition to providing service and repair work. They work on water piping systems, install fire protection sprinkler systems, and may also install, repair, or maintain hydronic (hot-water) heating systems.

Plumbers are in demand, and their compensation shows it. A survey of skilled workers in the construction industry alone found plumbers earning an average of $30.15 per hour, not counting fringe benefits.

If your concept of a plumber is the person who comes to your house to replace a leaking pipe or install a dishwasher, you may be interested to learn more about the role of plumbers. In construction, it is the plumber's job to install and repair the piping systems that carry water, waste, drainage, and natural gas in all sorts of buildings.

Working from blueprints or drawings that show the location of pipes, plumbing fixtures, and appliances, the construction plumber must lay out pipelines in a way that conserves materials but also meets stringent inspection requirements. These requirements vary depending on the type of building and the materials used, which may range from rugged plastic pipe to copper or cast iron. Sometimes the work requires cutting holes in

Plumbers install everything and the kitchen sink. Pictured here is a neotraditional style with integral apron front that recalls a bygone era (courtesy Kohler).

floors, walls, or ceilings. The plumber must cut, bend, and assemble lengths of pipe, using hand and power tools. This worker also makes piping connections, which usually requires knowledge of soldering techniques.

Construction plumbers need stamina to lift and carry tools and materials. They often stand, kneel, or crouch for extended times. The job may require working outdoors in extreme temperatures or in an unheated building. Sometimes the pipes are hot and the tools sharp. Such conditions require caution. Maintenance and repair work are other important aspects of plumbing. It is in this category that cross-training prepares plumbers to install and maintain heating or air-conditioning equipment or both.

Jobs range in size from the low-pressure boilers used to heat homes and small commercial buildings to room-size units that serve apartment complexes, schools, and shopping centers. Repair and maintenance duties generally include servicing appliances and equipment as well as maintaining piping systems.

HEATING TECHNICIANS/MECHANICS

Not all heating systems depend on circulating hot water. Heating equipment mechanics also install, maintain, and repair millions of systems that heat living spaces with forced air. Knowledge of various fuel sources is essential, ranging from oil, gas, and electricity to solid-fuel and multifuel systems. Such systems consist of many mechanical and electrical parts. Motors, pumps, compressors, switches, fans, ductwork, and pipes work together to generate and distribute the heat, then disperse combustion wastes.

Driven by new technology, the field of active and passive solar energy is having a greater impact in both space heating and cooling. It has both residential and commercial applications with which the plumbing/ HVAC workers of the future will work.

Regardless of the energy source, installation and maintenance technicians must be able to adjust system controls to work at the safest and most efficient levels. They must also test the performance of entire systems and diagnose and correct problems system-wide.

The ability to read blueprints or drawings is essential. Installation means more than setting the equipment in place. These workers must also install fuel and water supply lines, ductwork, and vents. They may be trained to connect electrical wiring and controls and check the system for proper operation. This requires the ability to use specialized equipment such as carbon dioxide and oxygen testers.

Many mechanics and technicians in these fields perform seasonal maintenance work and are subject to "busy" seasons. For heating specialists, this usually means the winter months. Air-conditioning and refrigeration mechanics encounter more "emergency" calls during the summer cooling season.

AIR-CONDITIONING TECHNICIANS

Speaking of air-conditioning and refrigeration, these workers install and service central air-conditioning systems and various types of refrigeration equipment. The latter are generally found in commercial and institutional settings.

Installation of systems is guided by blueprints, design specifications, and manufacturer's instructions. Mechanics and technicians work with motors, compressors, condensing units, evaporators, and related electronic and mechanical controls. They connect such systems and supply the necessary electrical power source, ductwork, and supply lines. Once installation is

An air-conditioning technician knows his way through the fence gates and narrow passageways of this central air conditioning unit. Service and maintenance calls are part of the work in this career (courtesy Bryant Corporation).

complete, they must charge the system with refrigerant and test it for proper performance.

Maintenance and repair are a significant part of this field. When equipment fails, technicians are called in quickly to diagnose the problem and make necessary repairs. Testing equipment helps to pinpoint trouble spots. During the off-season, many workers keep busy by performing routine maintenance or overhauling equipment.

On large projects, and in areas where union representation is prevalent, certain tasks are governed by trade union jurisdictions and can be carried out only by specific craftworkers. For example, ductwork may be fabricated and installed only by union sheet-metal workers; piping systems may be connected and installed only by union plumbers and pipefitters.

REFRIGERATION MECHANICS

Generally, the equipment on which refrigeration technicians work is more complex than air-conditioning units. These systems also cover a much wider range of temperature control. Temperature and humidity control, the filtration of clean air, and creation of special environments are all part of the modern refrigeration industry. For example, pharmaceutical and aerospace laboratories as well as hospital operating rooms require "clean-room" environments, free of even the tiniest airborne contaminants.

A journeyworker in refrigeration mechanics works from blueprints and verbal directions to install, maintain, and repair refrigeration and air-conditioning equipment and components used for living quarters, public areas, and industrial cold storage. A four-year apprenticeship is generally required to enter the trade, unless you have had equivalent practical experience. Such experience would include the layout, fabrication, and installation of refrigeration piping and tubing; the use of Freon refrigerants; the installation and repair of compressors, electric motors, fans, and blowers; pipe and tube bending; and soldering, handcutting, and threading of pipe.

Refrigeration equipment is installed and used in thousands of food processing plants, pharmaceutical labs, transport facilities, and even residential facilities such as nursing homes.

An important segment of the industry is the supermarket, with its long aisles of refrigerated cases and behind-the-scenes cold storage. Related to this segment are refrigerated transport trucks and container ships. To understand the possible work sites for refrigeration mechanics, estimate the number of supermarkets in your community, then multiply that figure by the number of towns and cities in the country.

Large store chains typically maintain their own technical crews, as do independent contract shops. With training and experience, you may choose to launch a business of your own. There are also opportunities in training, product distribution, and sales. The jobs of building operations and institutional refrigeration receive little publicity, but they are rewarding applications of mechanical skill.

Refrigeration mechanics may also repair or maintain the refrigerated containers used to ship perishable products. This is a relatively new development in marine refrigeration, but it has grown at a rapid rate. Most of the jobs are to be found in coastal regions, as are the shipbuilding and repair industries.

An insulated shipping box, often the size of a railroad car, can be loaded at a distant point and hauled to the dock by air, truck, or rail. These units typically use a mechanical refrigeration unit similar to that used for a truck or trailer body, although nonmechanical systems are also used. Utilized in fishing fleets, the units permit ships to stay at sea for weeks.

You may even take to the high seas in pursuit of your career as a refrigeration technician. Jobs are available on ships that carry perishable cargo or have a sizable crew living aboard for weeks at a time. Refrigeration is required to preserve food supplies and to provide air-conditioning in navigation and living quarters.

VENTILATION

The subspecialty of ventilation stands squarely in the middle of the industry abbreviation HVAC. Ventilation is defined as the exchange of air from indoors to outdoors through a system of vents or ductwork, generally ac-

Many mechanics and technicians in the fields of heating, cooling, and ventilation are very busy during their "seasons." The winter is this woman's busy season. She is adjusting heating equipment (© Impact Visuals/Rick Reinhard).

complished by a power source of some kind, and at a rate calculated according to the building's size and occupancy rate.

Based on what you already know about heating and cooling, you can understand the importance of good ventilation. In fact, building codes regulate these factors as a matter of public health and safety, particularly in air-conditioned buildings with sealed windows.

The formulas and guidelines required in building ventilation are taught as part of heating and cooling theory and practice courses. Calculating necessary air-handling ratios is at the core of this training. Public buildings are served by multipurpose systems that change the air in response to a programmed formula or time sequence, in addition to providing a source of heating or cooling or both. Providing adequate ventilation is primarily a matter of calculating the size of such units in relation to the space they serve.

SHEET-METAL WORKERS

Sheet-metal workers construct and install various types of ducts that are connected to form systems through which air passes. Most of the work discussed here includes the use of sheet-metal ducts in the HVAC systems of homes, commercial buildings, schools, hotels, ships, aircraft, and trains.

Generally a shop worker makes the ductwork according to plans based on the dimensions of a room or its heating and cooling system. A field person, sometimes called the "outside person," then installs the ductwork. Sometimes one person carries out both functions.

BUILDING MAINTENANCE/OPERATIONS

Some structures and building complexes are so large that their internal systems require a staff of skilled and semiskilled workers to operate and maintain. Such a crew is typically supervised by a chief engineer, whose duties are to plan and supervise all work on heating, ventilating, refrigeration, air-conditioning, electrical, and other mechanical systems. This person may also be responsible for the care of stationary engines, boilers, compressors, pumps, cooling towers and evaporative coolers, condensers, steam lines, water lines, and other piping-system components. A chief engineer must have extensive experience in working with this equipment at lower-levels jobs and in supervising other workers.

The maintenance field also provides many job opportunities for helpers, apprentices, journeyworkers, and supervisors en route to the title of chief engineer. Most supervisory jobs are filled from the journeyworker level by means of promotional exams, especially jobs in U.S. government facilities. In private businesses, promotions are made on the basis of merit and seniority. The requirements for education, technical training, and experience are similar, however. For more about opportunities for advancement, see Chapter 10.

A leader among professional groups associated with these trades is the American Society of Heating, Refrigeration and Air Conditioning Engineers (ASHRAE).

INTERRELATED SKILLS

As you can see, the service aspect of the plumbing, heating, ventilation, and air-conditioning/refrigeration trades requires a number of overlapping skills. Being a good service person is demanding; it requires that you think quickly to detect the part of a system that is malfunctioning. On the other hand, such work can provide a challenging experience for the right person.

When these industries expand and create new technologies, they also create opportunities for advancement. Because it is in their best interests to have workers available who have mastered the new technology, many of the industries provide career development in the form of workshops and seminars held at their own training centers and attended by instructors from vocational and technical schools in the region. These educators return to their classrooms with state-of-the art information. You could be the manufacturer's representative, the technical instructor, or the student acquiring new skills.

ENGINEERS AND ENGINEERING TECHNICIANS

Engineering technicians are usually graduates of a two-year associate program or a four-year program in a state or community college. Their work aids engineers in every step after the research process. To advance, a bachelor of science degree in engineering is generally required. Engineers who go into their own business often find a master's degree in business helpful. Because this field is constantly changing, continuing education is a way of life. Many engineering schools now have cooperative education programs that combine studies with practical experience in the job field. Taking part in such a program helps participants make career choices as well as financing their education.

There is a bright future ahead for engineers. This 20th-century career is evolving rapidly. Engineers have the chance to make human life better, so while the work is intellectually challenging, it is also fulfilling. Other rewards include good pay and plenty of mobility both within the field and geographically.

ENTREPRENEURS

These are good fields for the entrepreneur. The key is to acquire a good foundation of skills and experience, enhanced by sound management ability. Your goal is to establish a reputation for quality installation and service. To accomplish this, you need to find and then nurture capable employees who can perform the physical work and deal well with your customers. More information on these topics is given in Chapter 12.

WORKING FOR A MANUFACTURER

Earlier in this chapter, we mentioned Lennox International, Inc. as an example of a leading manufacturer of heating and cooling equipment. One of America's largest and most successful privately owned corporations, it has more than 7,000 employees worldwide. The Texas-based corporation has employment opportunities in both technical and nontechnical fields.

Here is a an overview of the job possibilities, with an emphasis on those that require a technical background:

accounting
aftermarket sales (coordinating sales of component
    parts and accessories)
customer financial services
customer service (handling calls from thousands of
    contractors who want to order HVAC systems
    and parts, or ask questions)
dealer development (working with dealers and
    contractors)
distribution and logistics
field sales
human resources
international export
law
management and information systems (computer-
    related)
manufacturing
marketing
materials
national accounts
public relations
quality assurance

Design, manufacture, installation, and repair of millions of home air-conditioning units such as this lightweight and quiet room-size model provide employment for thousands of trained technicians across the nation (courtesy Carrier Corporation).

research and development (approximately 200 engineers, technicians, and support personnel explore the future)

risk management

technical support (answering dealers' questions on product service and application).

An important factor in entry-level hiring at Lennox, according to Ruth Glover, employment specialist, is keyboard skills—the ability to enter data or call up information from a computer terminal. High schools increasingly view this training as a life skill, regardless of a student's career path.

Asked to discuss career opportunities at Lennox, Mrs. Glover cited customer service as a promising place to start. Such an assignment generally goes to a candidate with a two-year degree and some experience working in a technical field. For example, candidates often have a background in auto parts or electronics. Keyboard skills are important, she notes. Such a position offers workers a chance to learn about product distribution and how to work with customers.

Those who want to move up must expect to transfer, however. Among the skills they acquire is the ability to do "takeoffs"—a list of materials required to do a job. This list is based on the size of the house or building, for starters.

A new position at Lennox is the work of the inside sales representatives. These employees serve small accounts, mainly by phone, and enter orders via computer keyboard.

Territory managers deal with outside sales. Mrs. Glover noted that Lennox likes people in these positions to have a technical degree, plus a working knowledge of HVAC. Extensive travel goes with the assignment, but it is generally limited to overnight stays on the road. For example, on the densely populated East Coast a great many clients may be concentrated in an area. The territory manager may report to a district office, but not every day. Out West, a territory manager is likely to cover a wide geographic area with fewer clients. That situation would involve more time on the road. Promotion to regional sales manager is the next likely move. A customer service person could also advance by entering a manufacturer's marketing or credit department.

Multiply these career opportunities by the other manufacturing corporations in the industry, and the future looks even more promising for trained and talented workers.

WHERE THE JOBS ARE

Equipment manufacturers are usually located in cities, although wholesalers operate from regional centers across the country. Building and service contractors are scattered across the landscape, and there are franchised and independent dealerships in almost every town and city. In addition, government and utilities need their own staff or consulting personnel to keep systems running.

Now you know more about the work of these mechanics, technicians, and engineers. You have also glimpsed the employment opportunities that await in manufacturing and sales support. In the pages that follow, you will learn how to prepare for your career, what you will earn, and how to enter the world of work. Plenty of interesting, secure jobs are awaiting your consideration. To get started, just turn the page.

3

Historical Development

When did humankind develop piping systems capable of transporting water? Evidence exists today in the crumbling remains of the Roman aqueducts, but the story is even older, according to archaeological findings in Egypt, long held to be the cradle of civilization.

About 2500 B.C. the ancient city of Kish was known to flourish near the banks of the Euphrates River, where archaeologists were surprised to discover evidence of cemented tile drains and swimming pools. Further evidence that ancient civilizations used plumbing was documented on the Greek island of Crete, where indoor bathrooms were served by pottery pipes tapered to fit end-to-end. These facilities are also believed to date back to 2500 B.C.

The word "plumbing" derives from the Latin word *plumbum*, meaning lead, the metal frequently used by Romans to construct sanitary systems. Within the Roman empire, archaeologists have found prototypes of the modern water-flushed toilet. In and around the city of Rome, more than one thousand public baths have been excavated by archaeologists.

The Romans understood the concepts of masonry and hydraulics, as evidenced by the system of aqueducts they built for the transport of water over long distances. The Romans' ambitious political ventures took them into Europe, extending their empire as well as their plumbing theories. The Roman baths constructed over hot mineral springs in the English countryside are still in operation today, thousands of years after the Romans departed. The notions they transmitted concerning civilization extended to hygiene and cleanliness and were carried throughout the known world. A Roman colony in North Africa boasted what may have been the first public restrooms.

Unfortunately for humankind, the fall of the Roman Empire brought plumbing improvements to a virtual standstill. No significant developments occurred until the sixteenth century when an Englishman, Sir John Harrington, sought a patent for a water closet with a trap. His invention generated little enthusiasm, however, and another 200 years went by before a London watchmaker made improvements to Harrington's device. Indoor facilities were not widely accepted by the public until the development of public water supplies.

In the United States, it was the kitchen sink that led the way in acceptance of plumbing fixtures. Piped-in water eliminated the drudgery of carrying cooking water by the cumbersome bucketful. Bathtubs were the next commercial offering in indoor plumbing fixtures, the first designed simply of wood with a metal lining to prevent leaks. The first American patent for a water closet was granted in 1871.

The greatest advances in public sanitation came in the twentieth century, with many technical improvements and the development of long-lasting, reliable materials of metal, porcelain, and even plastics. Along with fixtures and piping products for individual buildings, modern plumbing systems relied heavily on development of municipal water and waste treatment facilities capable of meeting the needs of entire communities.

To assure the safety of public water supplies, plumbing codes have been developed. Such codes set the ground rules for plumbing design and quality of workmanship to avoid contamination of the fresh-water supply. The two most common health hazards related to plumbing involve cross connections and permitting the backflow of water. A cross connection results when undrinkable water is permitted to flow into the drinking-water system. Backflow is the result of creating a vacuum at a submerged water outlet by an excessive water demand from a lower level.

The water system for a single-family home served by a public utility follows a relatively simple design. A service pipe delivers potable (drinkable) water from the municipal system, conducted by pipes of various sizes and materials to fixtures throughout the home. A separate drainage system carries away waste water through horizontal pipes known as branches, or vertical piping (stacks). The piping material is generally of copper or, where codes permit, polyvinyl chloride (PVC plastic) for potable water. Drainage systems may be of cast iron, copper, steel, PVC, or lead.

Larger buildings, such as hotels, hospitals, or office complexes, are served by more complicated piping systems. It is likely that water pipes are accompanied by piping for steam, gas, compressed air, even oxygen and vacuum piping, depending on the building's use. The piping is generally grouped together within the walls. Access for repairs and maintenance is through panels installed at strategic locations.

Plumbing extends in scope beyond the design and installation of water pipes and drains. Plumbers are called upon to install and service natural gas lines for home heating, producing hot water, and operating appliances such as cooking ranges and clothes dryers. They may install the sprinkler systems used in fire protection, or piping systems to direct rainwater from roofs.

Plumbers are concerned with water treatment equipment including filters and softeners, along with the water supply and treatment systems for swimming pools and spas.

Pipefitters work with piping systems on a larger scale than the plumber ordinarily deals with. In industrial settings, at public utility installations, and at municipal water and sewage treatment plants, pipefitters build, maintain, and repair the piping used to convey water, natural gas, petroleum products, steam, or other substances. These piping systems may be designed to operate under high or low pressure. The job developed during the industrial age, when factories began turning to steam on a large scale, and in the case of petroleum refining, near the turn of the century, following the discovery of crude oil. As cities recognized the necessity of supplying clean water and the need to purify wastewater, treatment plants were built across the nation. Today, as communities grow and expand, new facilities are built. The existing facilities also require regular maintenance, updating, and expansion. The same is true for petroleum refineries and other industrial facilities that require large-scale piping systems for their operation.

Most pipefitters are union members, enjoying job security and generous fringe benefits.

Central Heating and Cooling Evolve

The heating, cooling, and ventilating industry has roots in the construction trades, particularly where large buildings are involved. The necessity to circulate air within a large structure, combined with what is today called "climate control" (heating and cooling), are reflected in the abbreviation HVAC.

Strange as it may seem today, there was a time when even multistory buildings were heated by fireplaces or freestanding stoves that burned coal. The invention of central heating permitted large spaces to be heated by a central source, usually located in the building's basement. Cities evolved "steam companies," which generated large quantities of steam heat and delivered it to customers through underground piping systems. In about the same time frame, natural gas and oil-fired boilers were developed in a size capable of heating large buildings by a network of radiators through which hot water was piped.

Imagine life without air-conditioning. Over the centuries, humans resorted to primitive means of getting relief from excessive heat and humidity—fans and blocks of ice among them. It wasn't until the early years of the twentieth century that an enterprising young engineer did for indoor climate control what Alexander Graham Bell did for communication and Henry Ford accomplished for transportation. An invention that was created to solve a specific industrial problem proved invaluable to humans at work and at home.

But first, a brief description of how it works: Air-conditioning is a process for controlling the temperature, moisture content, cleanliness, and distribution of air within a confined space. Perhaps our first idea of air-conditioning has to do with human comfort, but in a number of industrial processes indoor climate control is necessary for success. For example, textile mills need conditions of relatively high humidity, and multicolor printing plants must maintain constant temperature and humidity. Temperature and humidity control are also vital to most chemical processes. The air temperature must not exceed certain levels in facilities where computers are used, or sensitive electronic equipment may develop "glitches."

Air-conditioning can be credited to a single person, Willis Carrier, whose efforts to solve a printing plant's

Willis H. Carrier, the "father" of air-conditioning, hit upon the solution to a humidity problem in a Brooklyn printing plant (courtesy Carrier Corporation).

problems during the sweltering summer of 1902 led to an entire new industry. Today, Carrier Corporation is the world's largest manufacturer of indoor climate products.

As a young scientist, Willis Carrier was called to a New York printing plant to solve a longstanding summertime problem. The plant produced a popular color magazine, *Judge*, and changes in humidity wreaked havoc with the color printing process. Because of changes in the dimensions of the paper stock, the colors would not line up correctly. In printing terms, they were "off-register."

Carrier believed he could solve the humidity problem by "conditioning" the air, and he set about building a machine that would control both temperature and humidity by blowing air over artificially cooled pipes. Drawing on his engineering training at Cornell University, Carrier designed the unit's size and cooling capacity scientifically, based on the volume of air circulating in the plant. His invention was the world's first airconditioning system, a device that was to have a profound impact on the way people lived and worked.

Carrier is also credited with designing and installing the world's first residential air-conditioning system. Ironically, it was not in a steamy Southern locale, but in the Charles G. Gates mansion in Minneapolis, Minnesota, in 1914. That unit was twenty feet long, six feet wide, and seven feet high—considerably larger and less sophisticated than today's home air-conditioning systems.

That same year, the first hospital was fitted with airconditioning. Carrier's factory built and installed a unit for Allegheny General Hospital in Pittsburgh, Pennsylvania. The system was designed to introduce extra moisture into the air in a ward for premature

Luxury in bath design is a powerful force in today's home building and remodeling markets. This design showroom features a suite of fixtures and vanities known as the Trocadero Suite (courtesy Kohler).

infants. The device is credited with reducing infant death due to dehydration.

Central air-conditioning was not available on a wide scale until 1952, when it was introduced by a home-builder whom Carrier had persuaded to offer it as an option. Hundreds of curious people visited the model home in St. Louis, Missouri, to experience "climate control," and the event was even covered by *Life* magazine. Within two weeks, every home in the new subdivision was sold, complete with a central air-conditioning unit.

Air conditioners are designed to remove both heat and moisture from indoor air. Some buildings are equipped with dual-purpose units that also have a heating coil and humidifier for use in the cold season. Devices known as "air handlers" are capable of providing climate control under any seasonal condition: They contain a filter box to clean the air; both a cooling coil and heating coil to control temperature; a humidifier to control moisture, and a fan to circulate air in the room.

For many years, air-conditioning and refrigeration units were strictly mechanical. In an effort to bring down costs and increase efficiency, the latest product designs rely increasingly on electronic components. Although many employers still use the job title "HVAC mechanic," the designation "technician" is becoming a more accurate description.

As you might expect, these jobs exist throughout the United States, in small towns and urban areas. Cities and communities experiencing rapid population growth tend to offer the greatest number of new jobs, along with the best opportunities for apprenticeship training.

Once common primarily in the South and Southwest, residential air-conditioning is now popular throughout the United States. Those skilled in installing, repairing, or maintaining commercial refrigeration equipment can find work wherever there are restaurants, supermarkets, or even refrigerated transport trucks.

TODAY'S JOBS

Whereas pipefitters generally work for heavy construction companies or municipal utilities, plumbers and HVAC mechanics generally have more options in employment. Volume homebuilders may employ plumbing/HVAC crews directly or hire them on a subcontract basis. After gaining the training and experience required for journeyworker status, a number of these careerists opt for self-employment.

Plumbing shops that concentrate on service, repairs, and remodeling of installations are known as "kitchen and bath" operations. Because many heating systems involve the circulation of hot water through copper tubing, "plumbing and heating" are also common concentrations for small shops. Such operations often keep an HVAC mechanic on staff year-round. In industry terminology, yesterday's mechanics are becoming tomorrow's technicians, since the equipment they install, maintain, and repair is increasingly complex in design and construction.

Another source of jobs in the heating and cooling industry exists in manufacturing. Companies that design and make heating and cooling systems, in addition to those producing refrigeration equipment, are located throughout the continental United States. They need skilled workers in product design, quality control, production, and dealer service operations.

4

The Unions and Apprenticeship

In parts of the United States and Canada, most or all of the plumbers and pipe trade workers are represented by labor unions. Workers in the HVAC trades may also be union members, but the pipe trades have the largest number of union members. Being a member of a labor union offers a measure of job security and other important benefits, which begin with a worker's earliest days as an apprentice.

The purpose of a labor union is to negotiate with contractors (employers) on behalf of its members. Industry-wide agreements cover such important items as pay scales and working conditions.

As early as 1778, workers began banding together in efforts to secure better wages, minimum pay rates, shorter hours, apprenticeship standards for crafts, and the advancement of union labor. Workers who struggled to form craft unions did so in the face of stiff employer opposition as well as government interference. In fact, unions were prosecuted as "conspiracies in restraint of trade" under an old English common law doctrine. Still, by 1859 the Stonecutters, Hat Finishers, Molders, Machinists, and Locomotive Engineers all had founded national organizations. In Philadelphia, plumbers were active as early as 1827 in an organization known as the Mechanic's Union of Trade Organizations.

By 1850 plumbers had unions in Chicago, New York, and other cities along the East Coast. By the Civil War, there were gas fitters locals in Chicago, St. Louis, and New York. Within thirty years, the stage was set for development of a national pipe trades union. By 1883, the Association of Master Plumbers was already addressing an organized program of apprenticeship. After some early organizational hurdles were overcome, union workers formally banded together in a federation of locals in 1889. Within a decade, 189 locals were operating across the U.S. and Canada.

Known informally as the plumber's union, this respected force in labor carries the full name United Association of Journeymen and Apprentices of the Plumbing and Pipefitting Industry of the U.S. and Canada. You will also hear the name shortened to United Association or UA.

The decades following the Civil War represented an important era in the American labor movement. It was a time when fourteen new national unions were formed and the campaign for an eight-hour workday bore fruit. After years of interfering with labor unions, government finally began to make concessions on several major points. Congress adopted the eight-hour workday for federal employees in 1868.

Negotiations between the UA and employers have significantly raised the standard of living for workers. The workday and workweek have been shortened. Most agreements provide for health and welfare plans for workers and their families, and vacation and retirement benefits and paid holidays are now the norm. Safety remains a primary concern.

PAYING YOUR DUES

In return for union representation and services, members pay a one-time initiation fee and monthly dues.

Dues cover the costs of running the organization including salaries of union representatives, attorneys, research workers, and an administrative staff. Each union has officers elected by the membership and draws up bylaws reflecting grass-roots issues. Members run the union hall, deal with management on a daily basis, find work for members, and assign them to jobs.

To be eligible for membership benefits, a worker must keep dues paid up. Union members carry a dues book or card to confirm that their membership is in good standing.

APPRENTICESHIP

As mentioned earlier, most of today's union workers "graduated" to membership after completing a four-year apprenticeship sponsored cooperatively by union and industry partners. A United Association report cites a nationwide investment of more than $50 million per year in apprenticeship programs. Most local programs are locally financed. With such an investment at stake, it is not surprising that just one of every twenty apprenticeship applicants is accepted for training.

Qualifications may have minor differences from one geographic location to another, but basically an applicant must be of good moral character and physically able to perform the work of the trade; be between eighteen and thirty-four years of age; be a high school graduate or hold a GED certificate; hold a valid driver's license; and be a U.S. citizen residing within the geographic boundaries of the sponsoring local union.

Applicants pay a processing fee, generally about $20, and may be required to submit to a test for substance abuse.

The UA Apprenticeship begins with a six-month probationary period and is divided into one-year segments. Each segment consists of 1,700 to 2,000 hours of

35

on-the-job training and a minimum of 216 hours of related classroom instruction.

The classroom instruction is valuable; you must make up any work you miss before advancing to the next level of training. Apprentices work the same hours as journeyworkers, but they are barred from overtime if it conflicts with class schedules. For the most part, local conditions have a bearing on the number of hours designated for classroom instruction and which subjects are stressed. Instructors are usually UA members from the immediate vicinity. During the first years of training, all apprentices work under direct supervision of experienced journeyworkers. Later they may be allowed to work without direct supervision, but they remain under the jurisdiction of the Joint Apprenticeship Committee (JAC).

During the six-month probation, all apprentices are required to meet performance standards in on-the-job training and classroom instruction. This evaluation is based on the employer's report of progress, grades and attendance records in training class, and any disciplinary action taken against the apprentice. Those who make satisfactory progress are initiated into the local. An initiation fee is required, typically $500. Some unions require that half the sum be paid at the beginning of probation. Apprentices who fail to meet the standards are dropped from the program but have the right to a hearing.

The formal responsibilities that all apprentices must meet are stated in an agreement signed by the would-be apprentice and members of the JAC. The UA apprentice must agree to:

- Perform work and other duties diligently and faithfully in acordance with the provisions of the JAC's registered standards.

- Respect the property and abide by the rules and regulations of the contractor, the union, and the JAC.
- Attend classes regularly and complete the required hours of instruction.
- Maintain on-the-job records if required by the JAC.
- Develop safe working habits, and work in such a manner as to assure his or her safety and the safety of other workers.
- Behave at all times in a creditable, ethical, and moral manner.

The concept of training a new generation of pipe trades workers dates back to the 1880s. In an eloquent statement, members of the Master Plumbers' Association acknowledged that . . . "the craft owes society more than the labor of their hands; it owes the education of skilled workmen to follow after them in the same line of work, and to carry to great perfection the details of the craft."

To ensure that instructors were properly prepared for their task, the UA established a national training program at Purdue University in 1954. More than 22,000 instructors have attended the program, keeping up-to-date on new technical developments. Courses are tailored to the specific needs of the plumbing, steamfitting/pipefitting, and sprinkler installation crafts. Emphasis is not only on craft topics, but also on effective methods of teaching.

This chapter has focused on the United Association of Plumbers and Pipefitters; however, a number of HVAC workers belong to the Sheet Metal Workers International Association, which has headquarters at 1750 New York Avenue NW, Washington, DC 20006.

5

Other Routes to Training

Although most of today's plumbers and pipefitters and a good many sheet-metal workers choose a union apprenticeship as their route to the career field, a number of other training options are available for those who want to work in the plumbing/heating and cooling industry. Trade schools and community colleges offer programs of one to two years that lead to a certificate or associate degree in building technology. Those opportunities are described in Chapter 6.

For other routes to these career skills, consider that journeyworkers who have qualified as master plumbers by license or exam may hire and supervise the training of apprentices. In many heating and cooling businesses, a similar program of supervised on-the-job training transmits knowledge from one generation of skilled workers to the next. Many such programs include classroom instruction.

Apprenticeship programs are run by local chapters of several leading building trade associations. Look in the Yellow Pages for listings including:

- Associated Builders and Contractors
- National Association of Plumbing, Heating and Cooling Contractors (two programs, one union, one nonunion)

• Home Builders' Institute, educational division of the National Association of Home Builders.

Their programs are operated in cooperation with member businesses who actually hire and supervise the apprentices. The classroom hours are scheduled after or around the regular workday.

Some workers in the trades contend that "open shop" training is more valuable than the UA program to workers interested in residential and light commercial work, since it concentrates on those areas of study. The UA program spends more time on the "heavy industry" aspects of pipefitting.

As you can see, there are still jobs in the plumbing/ HVAC field for people straight out of high school. Often hired as helpers to start out, they are usually graduates with specific qualifications for the job. Good reading and math skills are necessary, as the work requires reading and understanding company manuals and work orders. Many companies use aptitude tests in the hiring process, measuring an applicant's abstract reasoning ability and mechanical aptitude. A physical ability test reveals balance, coordination, and strength levels. In heating, air-conditioning, and refrigeration in particular, some knowledge of basic electrical theory is helpful.

To understand how an informal apprenticeship works, consider a local contractor who is affiliated with the National Association of Home Builders. As a participant in the Home Builders' Institute Craft Skills Program (which has trained nearly 50,000 young men and women), you would be trained under the supervision of experienced craftsworkers, perhaps in a program called Community Revitalization. These cooperative ventures of local government and industry help workers acquire skills in the construction trades while rehabilitating a

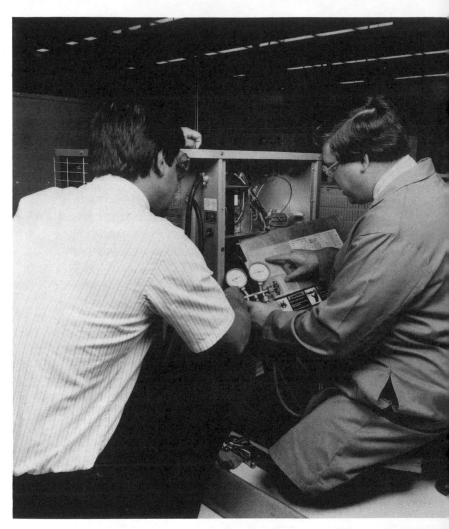

In an industry marked by technical advances, those who teach air-conditioning theory and practice must constantly sharpen their skills. An instructor at Carrier Corporation's Vocational Teachers Institute in Syracuse, N.Y., demonstrates refrigerant charging techniques. The two-week summer institute is held annually for professional HVAC instructors (courtesy Carrier Corporation).

community's housing resources. Completed projects are made available to low- and moderate-income families.

CAN YOU AFFORD TO LEARN?

As you ponder how to prepare for your career, you will most likely be concerned with limitations of money and time. Unlike many career fields, there are still ways to enter the plumbing/HVAC trades if either time or money is a problem. Through the Job Corps program, even people who left high school without graduating can get back on track while learning job skills. Concentrated on-the-job training lets you earn while you learn. Few people get a free education these days, and fewer still are paid to learn.

The Job Corps

For more than thirty years the Job Corps has offered basic education, vocational training, and job placement services to more than two million young men and women. This program and the P/HVAC industry got a boost in 1974 when the National Association of Home Builders joined forces to help train participants in construction trades. Among the eleven programs offered are plumbing, building and apartment maintenance, and solar heating installation.

Experienced journeyworkers prepare students to enter apprenticeship programs, to work with contractors and maintenance companies in entry-level helper positions, or to work in a plumbing/HVAC supply business as a counter salesperson. If you left high school before earning your diploma, the Job Corps can arrange a combination of high school and technical coursework to meet your needs. Classwork concentrates on preparing to take the GED, plus worker safety, tools and their use, blueprint reading, and practical work experience. Most courses are approximately 800 hours in length.

Statistics show that those who complete Job Corps training earn 52 percent more than those who do not finish training.

During training, Job Corps members live in dorms at the center and receive a stipend to cover basic expenses. The Job Corps offers graduates two distinct advantages: the skills and tools a professional needs, plus job placement assistance. To learn more about Job Corps programs, contact the state Job Service office in your community.

The Military

Enlisting in a branch of the U.S. military services is another way of training for a career in the plumbing/ HVAC trades. Combining job training with service to your country has proved to be a particularly satisfying approach.

Along with the chance to travel, military service gives veterans a leg up on attaining journeyworker status when they are discharged from active duty. The military pays a monthly stipend to veterans who take part in formal apprenticeship programs, and unions generally award advanced standing to veterans with P/HVAC training in their service record, reducing the time needed to earn a journeyworker's card.

Like all young people who enlist, you would take the Armed Services Vocational Aptitude Battery (ASVAB), a test that measures vocational aptitude and identifies areas of probable success in training.

As an example, here are details on the Air Force Heating Systems Specialist job classification:

This worker installs, modifies and repairs refrigeration, air-conditioning and ventilation equipment and systems. In addition, the worker installs mechanical, pneumatic, electronic and sensing/

switching devices designed to control flow and temperature of air, refrigerants or working fluids. Training enables the worker to connect wiring harnesses to electrical equipment; shape, size and connect tubing to components such as meters, valves, gages, traps and filtering assemblies using special bending, flaring and coupling tools and oxyacetylene torches for soldering and brazing; and conducts tests of installed equipment.

To do this work, candidates have had some or all of the following: courses in mechanics, machine shop, electricity and practical mathematics. Background may reflect specific mechanical aptitude, and/or work experience in a garage, power plant or machine shop.

To learn more about career opportunities in the armed forces, contact the nearest recruiting office or consult your school guidance counselor.

6

Schools and Home
Study Programs

Across the U.S. and Canada, trade schools prepare
workers for the building trades, including state-of-the-
art programs for future plumbers, refrigeration, and
HVAC workers. Some programs last ten months to a
year; others require two years. The longer programs
usually lead to an associate degree in building technology. The length of the program generally depends on
the content of the course. Plumbers and pipefitters take
a shorter course of study than those who must master
theoretical background along with practical aspects of
the career. For example, HVAC courses often include
electrical, mechanical, electronic, and design subjects.
Most of these programs take two years.

Learning the trade at a technical school is different
from apprenticeship in that you must pay for your
training. There may be an externship in which the
student works in a real-world situation, but unlike the
apprentice, you are not paid for your time or talent.

Students need to be cautious in choosing a school.
Quality instruction and the success of the school's placement service are important to question. Will you earn a
degree or certificate? What is the background of the
instructors? Is the school accredited? Do graduates get

good jobs quickly? Ask to speak with a recent graduate, or visit the school before signing up. There should be well-equipped workshops or labs with sufficient equipment for all students.

Be aware that there are both private technical schools and publicly supported community colleges. The latter may be the nation's biggest educational bargain, and they are well worth researching.

Most trade schools recommend that applicants have a high school background with at least one year each of general math, basic algebra, and science.

Upon completion of a year or two of specialized training, students are prepared to demonstrate technical skills in a variety of plumbing and HVAC applications. They apply accepted safety standards, meet work quality standards, and demonstrate knowledge of the specific trade. Early in their training, students learn to use and care for tools and materials. They learn to read and develop blueprints to perform installations that comply with the appropriate national code. Because communication is increasingly recognized as an important skill in the workplace, students are also expected to sharpen their writing and speaking skills. They must learn to interpret ideas and develop plans through communicating with others.

SUBJECTS YOU CAN EXPECT TO STUDY

Safety. This may be your single most important subject, regardless of the trade you choose. You must learn to use caution around tools and moving machinery parts. A central point is good housekeeping, since every mechanic, technician, operator, and plant engineer is responsible for the maintenance of clean, orderly, and safe workshops, machinery rooms, and storage areas. Students must understand the action and reaction of refrigerants, industrial gases, and other chemicals that may be exposed to extremes of temperature and pressure. Careless handling could result in a fire or an explosion.

Math. All of these crafts demand a good working knowledge of arithmetic and vocational mathematics. As a student and later as a worker, you will need to understand various formulas and constants to calculate areas of surface, contents of tanks, insulating factors, heat-load calculations, and others. Cost-estimating may be a daily requirement, another skill that relies on math. Basic applications of algebra and geometry accompany the technical work of HVAC.

Applied Science. Refrigeration and AC technicians and mechanics, operating engineers, and plant engineers need a solid background in practical chemistry and physics. This knowledge encompasses chemicals used for water softening, cleaning compounds, brine solutions, and other substances used to operate and maintain mechanical systems. Physics comes into play to measure heat and deal with such theoretical topics as strength of materials, electrical loads, and magnetism.

Communications. Clarity of thought and communication skills are needed to keep accurate records, logs, and daybooks. You may also be required to illustrate certain data with charts and graphs. Mastering this work is necessary to advance beyond an entry-level position. Often, technical workers are responsible for keeping records of plant operation, repairs, maintenance, and department activities. A daybook is a record of tasks assigned and completed, service calls, maintenance, and department needs. Operating engineers log equipment temperatures and pressures, humidity readings, and fuel consumption figures, among other data. A chief engineer needs knowledge and records of office procedures, shift schedules, and supervisory data.

SPECIFIC COURSE CONTENT

Plumbing

This one-year certificate program is typical of trade school curricula in various parts of the country. It includes the basic theories of plumbing, soil waste and vent layout, household and industrial maintenance, sewage systems, and the use of hand and power tools.

Students develop skills in all types of plumbing repair work used in residential, institutional, and commercial applications. The program also provides training in the fundamentals of communication and mathematics.

Courses in the first semester are Residential Plumbing, Introduction to Refrigeration, HVAC/R Electricity; Career Mathematics or Technical Algebra, and Trigonometry I.

The second semester consists of Commercial Plumbing, Practical Plumbing Experience, Blueprints and Specifications, Carpentry for the Trades, Communications or English Composition I, and Electric and Gas Welding.

At many technical schools, students who complete the plumbing program have the option of transferring into the HVAC technology degree program. This additional year of study can expand skills in air-conditioning and heating. The objective is to prepare students for entry-level jobs in plumbing. Graduates of the program should be able to:

- Demonstrate good work habits and meet accepted safety standards.
- Use hand and power tools of the trade.

47

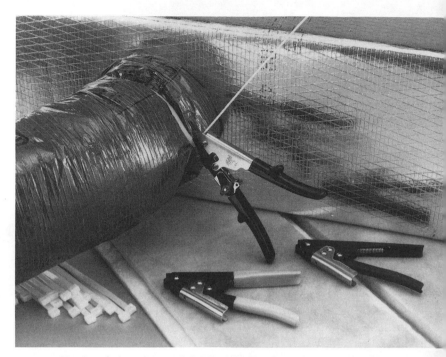

Tools of the air-conditioning trade. Pictured are a set of tie tools designed for setting heavy-duty nylon ties used in HVAC air handling systems (courtesy Malco Products, Inc.).

- Identify piping materials and install them, using proper connections.
- Know and apply trade terms and technical data.
- Read and interpret blueprints, specifications, and codes as they apply to the trade.
- Lay out, estimate, calculate, and use mathematical skills required in the trade.
- Install, maintain, and repair plumbing systems and keep up with developments in the field.
- Demonstrate ability to write letters of application, memos, work orders, and reports and apply communication skills on the job.

- Apply basic knowledge and skills of electrical work to install, repair, maintain, and troubleshoot electrical controls used in plumbing.
- Identify the principles involved in the collection, storage, and use of solar energy for space and domestic water heating.
- Apply energy conservation measures to plumbing installations.

Plumbing Skills, Residential—Covers the basic principles and skills used in hand and machine operations of the plumbing trade and a study of the materials and joining methods of various pipes used. Provides working knowledge of drain-waste-vent systems recognized by the National Standard Plumbing Code.

Plumbing Skills, Commercial—Covers basic principles and skills to install and maintain commercial and specialty plumbing fixtures and fittings, and regulations governing proper code installations.

Practical Plumbing Experience—Continues the study of blueprints, estimating, costing, and construction of plumbing projects. Construction projects on and off campus become available as jobs. Field trips to industries and businesses. Campus plumbing maintenance inspections.

Heating Systems and Design—Basic concepts and skills required to calculate, lay out, and design residential and commercial heating systems. Use of blueprints to calculate design and the layout of various heating systems to match structural designs for energy efficiency.

Basic Heating Systems and Design (Hydronics)—Basic entry-level skills required to calculate heat loss, design, and layout of various residential hot water central heat systems. Includes identification of boilers, systems, heating distribution units, and trim. System installation,

49

repair, and operation are covered, as well as natural gas piping, boilers, flue gas analysis, and combustion efficiency testing.

Hydronic Heating Systems—Basic entry-level skills required to identify, install, and operate residential and commercial steam heat systems, boilers, and trim. Emphasizes combustion efficiency testing, and oil and natural gas burner service, installation, and repair.

Plumbing for the Trades—Includes theory and laboratory assignments on basic residential plumbing. The fundamental principles of potable water distribution, drainage, waste, and vent systems. Common plumbing materials, fixtures, tools, shop equipment, and job safety are included. Methods and techniques of applying plumbing skills in the trade areas.

HVAC Technology

A typical community or technical college associate degree in HVAC Technology provides knowledge and skills training in air-conditioning, hydronic heating, temperature and humidity control, air circulation, duct and pipe system design and layout, thermostats, ventilating equipment, and automatic controls.

Classes are highly practical. Students learn to install and repair equipment in the lab segments of the program. The combination of lab practice and theory prepares students for employment and advancement in the heating, ventilation, and air-conditioning industry. Students are prepared for various jobs, including refrigeration and air-conditioning, heating (HVAC) equipment mechanic, estimator, sales representative, air-conditioning lab technician, industrial physical plant maintenance, and environmental control.

Recommended high school subjects include two years of algebra and a year each of science and physics.

First-semester topics include: Introduction to

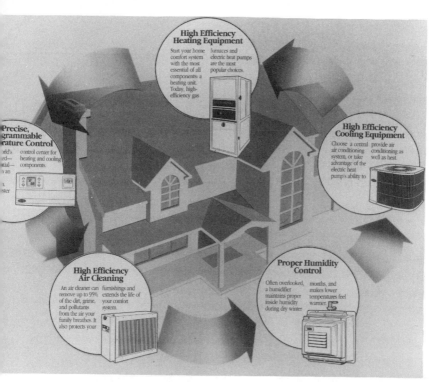

The whole is greater than the sum of its parts when it comes to indoor climate control. Pictured here is a modern, matched total system built around high-efficiency heating, cooling, humidifying, and air-cleaning units linked by electronic controls (courtesy Carrier Corporation).

Refrigeration, HVAC/R Electricity, Plumbing Skills (Residential), Career Math or Technical Algebra, and Trigonometry I.

Second-semester classes are typically: Blueprints and Specifications; Commercial Refrigeration Systems or Commercial Plumbing Skills, English Composition I, Fitness and Lifetime Sports; Refrigeration Emphasis or Carpentry for the Trades, and Plumbing Emphasis.

Third-semester courses cover: Basic Alternating Current Systems and Design, Residential HVAC

Controls, Basic Heating Systems/Design, Microcomputer Fundamentals, and a survey course in Physics.

Fourth-semester courses are: HVAC Systems II, HVAC Controls II, Commercial; Hydronic Heating Systems, Technical Writing, Humanities or Social Science elective.

Objectives of this program are to prepare students for employment in the field of commercial, residential, and industrial heating, cooling, and plumbing, and refrigeration installation, maintenance, and service.

A graduate of the program should be able to:

- Demonstrate the ability to do technical work in a variety of heating, cooling, plumbing, and refrigeration fields; apply safety standards; and understand and work with technical developments in the industry.
- Apply concepts of algebra and physics in the layout, design, development, and analysis of refrigeration and air-conditioning equipment and systems.
- Identify and demonstrate correct use of tools, materials, and equipment used in the trade.
- Demonstrate the ability to read and interpret blueprints and use them when installing equipment.
- Troubleshoot heating, cooling, and refrigeration equipment.
- Write clear, concise, legible, and accurate technical reports and apply verbal communication skills in job-related activities.
- Read and interpret electrical schematics and use schematics when installing and repairing equipment.
- Estimate the cost of an installation, and design

and lay out an effective system for a specific location and use.

- Demonstrate a responsible attitude in relationships with employers and coworkers and toward the world of work.
- Demonstrate an awareness of and respect for customer/employer relations.
- Demonstrate knowledge of the operation and use of hermetic, reciprocating, and centrifugal compressors.
- Apply basic knowledge of air flow, ventilation, and energy conservation concepts, the design of systems using modern building design, and solar energy technology.
- Install, service, and repair hydronic heat systems, controls, and heat distributing units.
- Install and troubleshoot residential and commercial electrical, pneumatic, and electronic HVAC control systems.
- Use microcomputers to design, monitor, and control HVAC systems in commercial buildings.
- Demonstrate a knowledge of gas and oil-fired boilers and heat pump installation and service.

Refrigeration Technology

Refrigeration technology students learn about system design and operation with an emphasis on commercial and motor vehicle refrigeration systems. Installation and service procedures are generally emphasized. Certificate programs may be one year in length; associate degree programs require two years.

Typical course offerings include:

Introduction to Refrigeration. Introduces the student to basic refrigeration systems. Proper and safe use of tools, identification of materials, methods of assembling

53

refrigeration systems, and proper handling of refrigerants are included. Emphasis is placed on basic system components, evaporators, compressors, condensers, and test equipment.

Blueprints and Specifications. Introduction to blueprint reading for plumbing, air-conditioning, and HVAC in residential and commercial applications. Includes specifications, symbols, and information contained on construction drawings.

Commercial Refrigeration Systems. Introduction to commercial refrigeration systems, different types of refrigeration systems and their methods of operation. Understand and identify the types of controls required to control temperature, humidity, air circulation, and defrost procedures.

Commercial Installation and Service. Skills required to recognize and correct installation errors and service problems in commercial refrigeration systems. Troubleshooting of mechanical and control malfunctions as they relate to the operation of commercial refrigeration systems.

Basic A/C Systems and Design. Basic entry-level skills required to identify, install, and operate various central A/C systems for residential and light commercial installations. Basic concepts and skills required to control temperature, humidity, air circulation, and defrost procedures. Includes skills required to calculate, lay out, and design residential cooling systems. Basic skills in the layout and fabrication of one-inch fiberglass ductboard, to include straight duct, offsets, and 45-degree and 90-degree elbows. Review of the proper handling and use of the types of refrigerants covered by the Clean Air Act and the Montreal Protocol.

Commercial Installation and Service. Focuses on the ability to recognize and correct installation errors and service problems, including trouble-shooting mechanical and control malfunctions in commercial refrigeration systems.

INDEPENDENT STUDY OPTIONS

The Refrigeration Service Engineers Society offers ten 72-hour courses conducted at local chapters. This world-wide association has some 400 local chapters and 29,000 members primarily engaged in servicing domestic, commercial, and industrial refrigeration, air-conditioning, and heating equipment. It is a nonprofit educational association devoted to improving technical abilities of members, encouraging ethical standards, and stimulating individual growth. Write to: RSES International Headquarters, 960 Rand Road, Des Plaines, IL 60016.

If there are no schools near you, and you can't afford to go away for training, consider a home study or correspondence course. In less than one year of your spare time, you can earn a career diploma in plumbing/HVAC by completing a series of lessons and practical projects designed by experts in independent learning. As with any training course, you should make a careful investigation before signing up. In the best courses, students use the same textbooks as in on-campus courses, carrying out projects that are evaluated by well-trained instructors.

Many people who have highly successful careers learned through a combination of home study and OJT. This training requires serious motivation and the ability to meet deadlines. Those who have problems in these two areas may have difficulty without the structure of the traditional classroom. Several correspondence schools offer faculty support through toll-free telephone hotlines to assist students with their studies.

A number of leading industrial corporations pay to have their employees take home study career training. Among them are *Fortune* 500 companies, leaders in the chemical, transportation, paper, petroleum, and mineral industries.

For information on an industry-approved course, contact ICS School of Air Conditioning/Refrigeration, 925 Oak Street, Scranton, PA 18515.

SKILL IMPROVEMENT PROGRAMS

As in most careers in the information age, new techniques and materials bring change to the plumbing/ HVAC fields. Those who want to grow with the industry must keep pace with new developments. Advanced skill improvement programs fill that need. Short courses that concentrate on a specialized area are designed for workers who have advanced beyond the apprentice level. Technical knowledge acquired in such classes is often the basis for advancement to a supervisory position. This is a primary method by which journeyworkers can develop expertise in a special area. Courses may be sponsored by product manufacturers, a contractor's association, or a government agency.

PUTTING A TECHNICAL DEGREE TO WORK

The person who earns a two-year technical degree, generally called an associate degree, is likely to have higher earnings and wider career opportunities after just two years on the job. This level of education is in demand. Employers assign these graduates to such jobs as engineering assistant, sales engineer, drafter, estimator, building engineer, plant engineer, and lab and field service technician. Some graduates work a few years for an employer before striking out on their own as an independent contractor. At some point in their career, many people decide to continue their education. It is possible to apply the credits earned in an asociate degree to many four-year programs. Graduates of certificate programs may be awarded advanced placement at college.

For example, many technical backgrounds can be the foundation for a degree in mechanical engineering. Employers often pay some or all the costs of completing a degree.

Learning is a lifelong process for those with ambition and a curious mind. Education is never wasted, and it may pay surprising dividends in the future.

7

Opportunities for Women and Minorities

The years ahead hold remarkable promise for women and minority workers seeking a career in the blue-collar trades. By 1999, the construction industry alone should be offering one of every three new jobs to a minority or woman worker. The trend began slowly in 1978, when Title 29 of the Equal Employment in Apprenticeship legislation was adopted, and it has been growing steadily ever since. Within five years of enactment of the legislation, minority placements exceeded 20 percent, and women attained an increase of nearly 4 percent.

Apprenticeships, whether union or open shop, are regulated by the U.S. Department of Labor, which insists that a certain percentage of available slots be awarded to women and minorities.

Because the plumbing/HVAC trades command good pay and are in demand, it is no surprise that many women and minority candidates seek careers in these fields. Several factors should keep the employment gates open and ever-widening. Government supervision of industry hiring practices is a major influence. Contractors who bid on government contracts are already working with target figures in hiring. Enlightened attitudes on the part of unions and employers are taking effect, and the explosion of myths about gender and the nature of work are having a significant impact. As the building trades compete for the best and brightest among a new generation of workers, salary increases and more attractive working conditions will result.

Later in this chapter is an interview with two women who founded their own plumbing and heating business, Pipelines, in the Greater Boston area. Although the work can be arduous, it has many rewards. As leaders in a pioneering era of nontraditional work, Maura Russell and Christine Ernst are helping to train a new generation of workers. Their thoughts and ideas help clarify what it is like to work in a nontraditional field.

The federal Job Corps program has trained more than two million young people, including women and minorities, for nontraditional careers. Plumbing and building maintenance are among the eleven building trades taught at Job Corps centers across the country.

"STEP-UP" PROGRAMS

To prepare young people for apprenticeship, a network of "step-up" programs has been established across the country, giving instruction in the basic skills and workplace attitudes necessary for success.

The following is a capsule view of several such programs. To find one near you, look in the telephone directory for the Job Service office, YWCA, National Association of Women in Construction (NAWIC), or Job Training Partnership Administration office.

The National Association of Women in Construction maintains a number of regional chapters that have banded together to offer a program known as PACTT (Preliminary Awareness of Construction Trades Training). This eight-week program is a hands-on exploration of four construction trades: carpentry, electrical, masonry, and plumbing. Since residential and light

59

commercial plumbing often involve basic knowledge of carpentry and electrical work, this is a well-balanced introduction.

Participants learn about the industry and apprenticeship, acquire a vocabulary of construction terms, learn how a job progresses from beginning to end, and study such related topics as blueprint reading, craft math, tool care and safety, and clothes and equipment for the job site. In addition, there is instruction on job interview skills, handling sexual and racial harassment, and building physical stamina.

Students are provided with a mentor who tracks their progress during a follow-up period. The program is available in a number of cities in the U.S. and Canada. For additional details, call NAWIC toll-free at 1-800-552-3506. NAWIC headquarters is at 437 South Adams Street, Fort Worth, TX 76104.

With more than 8,500 members, the National Association of Women in Construction is a strong voice for nontraditional workers from apprentice to contractor. It provides job referrals for members, takes part in career recruitment, shares industry knowledge and ideas, and offers construction education opportunities, including scholarships for women preparing to enter the industry.

The National Association of Home Builders is well aware that one of every three new construction workers in the decades ahead will be female or a member of a minority, since it was this trade association's research that uncovered the fact. The NAHB recruits both women and minorities for its Craft Skills Program, directed by the Home Builders' Institute, the education and training division of NAHB. Local programs are run by more than 100 participating building contractors. Practical in nature and offering the latest in tools and technology, the HBI program offers a gateway to the trades for more than 50,000 young men and women.

Established in 1990, the *National Tradeswomen's Network* is a group of organizations and individuals committed to increasing the numbers of women entering nontraditional blue-collar occupations. The NTN's goals are to affect national policy, enforce and expand affirmative action standards, support and promote regional and local NTN efforts, promote a safe environment and quality workplace, and challenge gender-based work and educational policies. National headquarters is at 37 South Ashland Avenue, Chicago, IL 60607.

Other groups working on these goals include such organizations such as *Chicago Women in Trades*, *Women in the Building Trades*, and the *Coalition of Labor Union Women and Tradeswomen, Inc.* Many sponsor training programs or distribute free information. To find the group nearest you, consult the telephone book or inquire at the women's center, vocational-technical school, or local Chamber of Commerce and Industry.

The national network of *YWCAs* has a long tradition of assisting women in seeking more challenging, better-paying employment. More than a century ago, YWCAs took on the task of teaching women to type at a time when such work was considered "too demanding" for them. Current efforts focus on identifying job opportunities, recruiting women workers, and providing support services. You can find the nearest YWCA in the telephone directory.

Wider Opportunities for Women, Inc., popularly known by its initials—WOW—is an effective agency based in Washington, DC. The twenty-week program it operates focuses on a combination of practical work topics, job search skills, and life skills. Craft math, communications, and internships are included.

Participants are readied for entry-level jobs in building maintenance and repair or entry into an apprenticeship program. Life skills include such topics as assertiveness

This electronic air cleaner filter has just undergone an easy cleaning procedure in an automatic dishwasher, eliminating the need for replacement. Modern air cleaners dramatically reduce indoor grime and save money and time spent cleaning walls and furnishings (courtesy Bryant Corporation).

training, decision-making and goal-setting, coping with family and work demands, dealing with stress, time management, maintaining health, sexual harassment in the workplace, and keeping a good job. A combination of trade skills are covered, ranging from carpentry, electrical work, and painting to heating system repairs and residential plumbing.

The program operated by *TREE* (Training, Recruiting, Educating and Employing, Inc.), based in Edison, New Jersey, also focuses on the trades for anyone eligible under JTPA regulations and residing within the three counties the agency serves. Plumbing topics covered include venting and draining, installation of pipes, and venting systems. The eight-week program prepares students to enter apprenticeship.

Another New Jersey program, *PREP* (Pre-apprenticeship Entrepreneurial Training for Women), includes heating, air-conditioning, and ventilation in twelve weeks of intensive training. The program is open to residents of Sussex County having a high school diploma or GED.

In Oakland, California, *Women in the Skilled Trades* (WIST) offers training in carpentry, sheet metal, welding, electrical, basic machining, and pipe trades. Classes in math and English are geared to workplace situations. Also offered are skills training, physical education, life skills, and hands-on experiences such as building, tearing down, and repairing building systems.

The *Portsmouth Naval Shipyard* in Kittery, Maine, operates a four-year apprenticeship program that trains women and men to overhaul nuclear submarines. Pipefitter is among the six occupations taught in on-the-job training. From a class of 200, 20 to 25 students are women. A strong aptitude for math is a requirement.

Similar programs are operating in all fifty states. For additional details, contact one of the ten regional offices of the U.S. Department of Labor's Women's Bureau, or request a copy of the Directory of Non-Traditional Training and Employment Programs Serving Women. Single copies are free of charge and may be obtained from the U.S. Department of Labor, Women's Bureau, 200 Constitution Avenue NW, Washington, DC 20210-9990.

Although women are the primary target group of the programs described here, most are also open to men seeking job training. Often, the funding grants that support the program define the target group as displaced homemakers, single parents, or dislocated workers.

Another valuable resource in minority job-training is the *Labor Education Advancement Program* (LEAP) of the National Urban League. For details on this program, contact the League at 500 East 62nd Street, New York, NY 10021.

Other groups working toward fuller employment in the trades are the following:

Associated Minority Contractors of America
1329 E Street NW
Washington, DC 20004

Coalition of Labor Union Women
15 Union Square
New York, NY 10003

National Association of Minority Contractors
1750 K Street NW
Washington, DC 20006

National Resource Center for Minority Contractors
1705 DeSales Drive NW
Washington, DC 20036

TWO WOMEN WHO ARE MASTER PLUMBERS

Lights! Action! Camera! This was no ordinary day on the job for the two master plumbers from Boston. A TV crew from the public broadcast network home improvement show "This Old House" was filming them at work on a renovation project.

Partners in a corporation known as Pipelines, Maura Russell and Christine Ernst are part of a growing network of women succeeding in nontraditional blue-collar careers. Their appearance on national TV was not because they are women plumbers, but because their firm was the successful bidder on a job that included replacing a heating system and renovating a bathroom, kitchen, and laundry.

During the TV segment, viewers see Maura assembling and installing the PVC piping and fittings for a bathroom sink, work that eventually would be hidden behind a wall. When the camera cuts away to an interview with Christine, she is in the basement, taking notes for the design of the new heating system. Just a typical day for a couple of entrepreneurs with a quarter century of working experience between them.

Later, in an interview for this book, Russell explained that they got the job when the project's kitchen designer asked them to bid. The home's owners had seen the work Pipelines had done on another job and were interested in the sort of careful, expert work for which the firm is known.

Pipelines is also known for supporting the efforts of nontraditional workers seeking training. As master plumbers, the business owners can hire and supervise apprentices. Two of their former apprentices have launched businesses of their own, and another is planning to go solo in Vermont. Maura Russell's résumé includes a stint as a vocational school teacher who instructed adults and high school students in pipe trades.

How did this Smith College graduate with a degree in government choose to enter the plumbing and heating business?

"I was always interested in how things worked," she explains. She took a year off between junior and senior year of college to earn some money. The best money turned out to be from a job as a welder in a shipyard. "I found I liked working in metal, and my studies of women's history showed there was a small window of access open to nontraditional careers."

A combination of factors led her to apply for a union apprenticeship program. At a time when just one of every twenty applications was approved, Maura was accepted and stayed two years, until she realized that her real interest was in residential and light commercial work. "The union training was geared more toward large construction and pipefitting, so I finished my apprenticeship in a nonunion shop." In total, apprenticeship required 6,000 hours of on-the-job training, plus 300 hours of classroom instruction. To secure a journeyworker's card, she had to pass a practical licensing exam.

The double goal of starting a business and teaching the trade to others prompted Maura to tackle the master's rating. The first requirement was to have three years of journeywork, plus another 150 hours of classes and a skills test.

For Christine Ernst, becoming a partner in a plumbing and heating business was less of a conscious choice. She won a slot in a UA apprenticeship program in 1981, when affirmative action guaranteed women access to the training.

Completing the apprenticeship meant receiving a journeyworker's card and working out of the union hall in Springfield, Connecticut, at the start of her career. A job sent her to Boston, where she decided to stay. Construction activity eventually slowed, and she was among union plumbers furloughed. "I started working for myself then. After all, there's just so many years you can stay interested in core-boring holes for hotel foundations."

Ernst had seen how specialized some of the union jobs could be, citing examples of workers "who didn't know about simple things like faucet washers, because they had spent their entire worklives connecting large pipes."

Convinced that it was time for a change, she went independent. Having a partner meant some relief from the pressure of emergency repair calls, and they were able to bid larger, more time-consuming projects. Much of Pipelines' work consists of residential and commercial remodeling. They also handle maintenance and service on heating systems and water lines. While the partners handle the day-to-day business and bookkeeping details, they contract out such accounting functions as tax reports.

Communication is a vital part of the business for working partners. A combination of electronic voice mail, answering machines, and pagers currently meets their needs. The business requires communicating with clients, suppliers, contractors, and the workforce.

"If you get into a job and discover that suddenly you need another set of hands, it's convenient to call someone in," Maura points out. Pipelines' clients also find it reassuring that they get a prompt return call, even when the plumbers are busy with another job.

Admitting that the work requires a certain level of physical stamina, Russell said there is not a great deal of heavy lifting. In a metropolitan area, suppliers are willing to deliver items such as boilers and water heaters. "I drive a light van and carry all the tools and a small supply of fittings that you need for most calls."

Like other successful companies, the owners of

Pipelines have discovered that meeting the needs of customers is essential.

"We've found that elderly people often prefer to have women working in their homes. Personal security is a big issue for them—you know, having strangers in their homes, walking around carrying pipe wrenches. There seems to be a sort of informal referral system at work. One person needs some work done, and another client recommends us, so we get the call. It's important to be patient with clients, to hear them out and explain things fully so they understand what has to be done, what it will cost, and how long it will take. I'm not sure everybody in the business takes this approach, but we do."

Another aspect of Pipelines' customer service has to do with tidiness. "Care and attention always take a few moments longer, but it's worth it. I like to know the job is done the best way possible, because it's going to be there a long time. And it's not visible; if something goes wrong, it's hidden in the wall, where a leaking pipe can cause serious structural damage if it goes undetected."

Admitting that most of their customers never see the stark beauty in a job done well, Russell does recall the time they were working on a commercial building that was to house an art gallery. The piping was all copper, to meet building code, and "it was actually beautiful. One of the artists recognized that quality and admired the artistry of the work, saying it was a shame to cover it with a wall."

Still, this is a job where workers get dirty. "A few of my friends have seen the way I look after a tough day, and they say they couldn't stand to get so dirty," Ernst observes. "But there are rewards for the grimy times. We've also had the occasional carpenter on the job complain a little about how much we earn. My response is to get out on your own and work for yourself. You take the risk, you reap the reward."

Maura Russell notes that it is the opportunity to choose the people with whom you work, doing jobs that you choose, that makes the work satisfying. "Most jobs don't offer that degree of personal choice," she adds.

Would she recommend the career to her young nieces? "It's a great trade. You can make a good living, and the work gives you exposure to many trades—a little carpentry, some electrical work—and you get to work in a variety of settings."

She sees the career as a good opportunity for a single parent, too, since the hours can be quite flexible.

Possessing a career skill that is in demand has proved to be a source of security and satisfaction to them both.

"When someone has no heat, it makes me feel good to know I can solve that problem," Maura says. "For example, on Thanksgiving Day my next-door neighbors were cooking like mad, the kitchen full of dirty dishes and a houseful of company on the way. Then a pipe broke in the attic and suddenly—no water! I was just a phone call away and in very little time was able to solve the problem for them."

Christine has also had occasion to be the "problem solver." As a house guest, she never worries about a gift for her hosts, since "when you go to visit people, there's invariably a faucet dripping or some such problem. I just take along a small toolbox and fix it. People really appreciate that kind of thoughtfulness."

The partners both cited the same frustration in their work, and it is a problem that plagues most professionals—bidding an installation job. "We are very meticulous in our approach to bidding," Maura explains. "We spend a lot of time and effort to match the equipment to the owner's heating needs. We go from room to room measuring, and spend time interviewing the homeowner to determine the best match between the systems available and the life-style of the people who will be using it.

"Maybe our bid will end up $50 higher than the company that just measured the outside of the house, or plans to stick in the same size boiler that was there before, whether or not it's economical for the homeowner to operate for the next twenty-five years. The customer takes the lower bid, for whatever reason, because he doesn't understand the fine points, or because it's a little cheaper. That's very frustrating."

Christine agrees that estimating jobs is difficult, but adds that billing is another challenge.

"Valuing your work correctly and getting paid for your work. Those are the hard parts."

As business owners, where do they see Pipelines going in the future?

"Within five years, hopefully, we'll have a larger group of people working for us and in training," Ernst responds. During an interview from her suburban Boston home, Russell agrees, recalling that "window of opportunity" for women in the trades that she described earlier. "I'd like to see Pipelines get a littler larger, with more apprentices."

While the time required to film segments of their work for "This Old House" cut into their work schedule (therefore affecting the profit margin on the job), Russell and Ernst agreed to the filming because both feel it is important to have more visibility for women in the building trades. More than a decade after affirmative action plans guaranteed access to training, there are still very few women pursuing careers. In all of New England, there may be as few as half a dozen shops operated by tradeswomen.

8

Wages and Benefits

The simple economic truth is that people are paid varying rates for their labor and expertise within a given industry. This situation exists for a variety of reasons. Geographic factors, supply and demand, union or independent, experience levels, the nature of the work being performed, the size of the business one works for, and even the relative affluence of the community being served—all of these details have an impact on wage scales.

Traditionally, members of craft unions and those who work in the construction trades lead the salary parade. As you might expect, union construction plumbers are the most generously compensated of all workers in the plumbing, heating, and cooling industry. Construction workers are also exposed to the greatest financial and safety risks of the trades, which is reflected in their pay scale. Inclement weather, downturns in the economy, and downtime between jobs can mean interruptions in earning power, for which higher hourly wages are intended to compensate. Often, these workers do not receive paid holidays or vacation time, another compensating factor.

The geographic influence on wage scales has been a longstanding situation, but one that union bargaining is currently addressing. Traditionally, areas in the

71

Southeastern and South Central states have lagged behind the national average in pay scales, but most often the cost of living in these areas has likewise been lower. For example, it is easier to make ends meet on $12 an hour where housing costs average $400 per month than where rents average $550.

Another problem arises in discussing wages and benefits in this industry. It is difficult to track wages because of the mix of union and nonunion workers and the combination of construction, maintenance, and installation operations. In some parts of the country, plumbers also install heating systems but have nothing to do with air-conditioning. In others, plumbing and cooling are closely aligned operations, and cross-training of workers is an accepted feature of the industry. Some "kitchen and bath shops" are closely aligned with carpentry and remodeling operations, whereas pipefitters and sheet-metal workers may exist in virtual isolation from other facets of the industry.

In addition, wage reports vary in timeliness. Here's an example. Because it uses a newsletter format that requires little time in production, the Construction Labor Research Council can produce a report in February on the previous year's wage and benefits figures for the sixteen trades it monitors. In contrast, the hardcover *Occupational Outlook Handbook* contains statistics that are a year old or more when the book goes to press. The same is true of other career research books.

In addition, some books report earnings and their variables as highs, medians, and lows for the overall industry. Others report by job category. Some consider heating, air-conditioning, and ventilation workers as a single unit; others do not. The result makes for difficult reporting.

In reading this chapter, be aware of the "patchwork quilt" nature of reporting wages in this industry. A

Modern plumbing and heating supply dealers display their wares in settings aimed at catching the eye of consumers. Visitors to home shows are attracted to this exhibit of the Mastershower Tower, featuring multiple water functions controlled by a push-button panel (courtesy Kohler).

simple comparison of figures is not readily available, but a careful analysis of the statistics will provide the information needed to understand the earning potential in these trades.

THE PLUMBING TRADES

Union plumbers earn among the highest wages in the industry. Within this group, construction plumbers and pipefitters are the leaders.

The Construction Research Council reported union wages and supplements at the end of 1993 as $32.99 for plumbers; $28.76 for pipefitters; and $28.01 for sheetmetal workers. Of course, these were workers employed on construction projects. Total earnings packages often included various fringe benefits. In some cases, the fringes were paid by the employer, in other cases, by the union. Typically, they included vacation and holiday pay, health insurance, and pension plans.

Union workers are paid overtime wages at a scale of $1\frac{1}{2}$ times the hourly scale after the regular workweek (from 35 to 40 hours, depending on contract terms). Under certain circumstances (Sunday or holiday work, for example) they may earn twice the hourly wage.

Plumbers who work for small business operators (fewer than twenty-five employees) in the kitchen and bath remodeling category typically earn between $18 and $25 per hour. Fringe benefits vary from shop to shop, depending on factors stated earlier. Wages tend to be higher along the densely populated East Coast and in California. The lowest wage scales are seen in the South Central and Southeastern states. Similar wage scales were reported for the independent plumbing repair shops and operations that focus on light commercial installation and repairs.

HVAC WORKERS

Like other careers in this industry, wage scales reflect not only geographic factors but also the level of training and expertise of the worker. To learn the trade, these workers devote several years to technical school, apprenticeship, or on-the-job training. Their financial rewards reflect this investment. In the future, wages are expected to rise as the result of a worker shortage. The number of workers nearing retirement age is on the increase, and employers must meet the challenge of filling these positions. Increased wages are one of the most effective recruitment strategies.

According to the U.S. Department of Labor, median weekly earnings for technicians in the air-conditioning, heating, and refrigeration industries were $447 in 1990. This figure has probably increased by 6 to 10 percent. The term *median* means that half of all workers earned more than this sum, and the other half less. The top salaries paid exceeded $775 per week in 1990.

Fringe benefits generally encompass paid vacation and holidays, health insurance, and frequently participation in a pension plan. Some companies provide a truck or van, uniforms, and pay for skills improvement training.

Because of the technical nature of their work, technicians who install, repair, and maintain air-conditioning equipment are in demand, particularly in temperate climates. Half of all such workers were earning about $450 per week in 1990, and top wages were reported close to double that figure. These U.S. Department of Labor figures reflect wage and salary workers, excluding the self-employed. Some of those reporting do a combination of heating and cooling work; some specialize in air-conditioning, others in refrigeration technology.

Unlike the union construction wage report, these figures on HVAC technicians are not broken down by

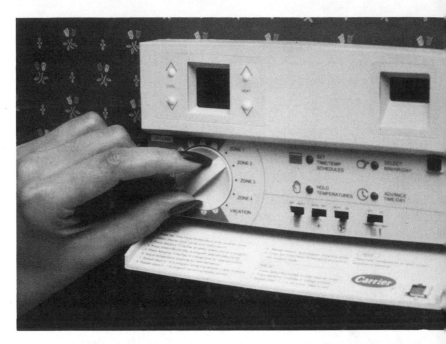

The latest in whole-house comfort is controlled from this tiny electronic panel, capable of establishing four different heating or cooling comfort zones within a home. Families can program the zones individually after installation by a P-HVAC professional (courtesy Carrier Corporation).

geographic region. Typical fringe benefits include health insurance, pension plans, paid vacations, and holidays. These workers often drive a company van or light pickup truck and have the use of specialized tools provided by the employer.

Because the work is highly technical and subject to changes in the industry, continuing education and job training are important. Employers generally cover the expense of such training for their workers, viewing the investment as part of the cost of staying competitive.

Stationary engineers, whose work is detailed in Chapter 10, are generally paid on an hourly basis, plus fringe benefits. The 40-hour week may require weekend and holiday schedules. Wage rates cited here are based on the Department of Labor's 1990 figures and have increased approximately 6 to 10 percent. The average wage in metropolitan areas was $16 per hour, with Western locales leading at $18.49 per hour in 1990. The lowest wages were reported in the South, at $13.88. The top 10 percent earned more than $937 per week.

A key element in career planning is to match the type of work you want to perform with the level of earnings you want and need. As you get closer to the day when you will launch your own career, remember to check on wage increases in the industry. This information can be obtained from government and industry sources, many of which are listed in the Appendix of this book.

Entering the World of Work

_9_

No matter how much care and attention you give to learning about a career in advance, professional job counselors agree that you cannot be one hundred percent certain that you will like a job. Sometimes actual work experience is the only way to learn for sure. Still, you can improve the odds by asking yourself some realistic questions.

For example, how is your overall health? As a group, blue-collar workers are healthier than the general population, and it's a good thing, considering the strenuous tasks they are often asked to perform.

Are you willing to take a complete physical exam? Most hirings depend on the results of such an exam. If you are hesitant, it will reduce your chances of being hired. Also, many employers require random drug screenings as part of their hiring process.

Do you have reliable transportation? Even if your employer provides a light truck or van for service calls, you will be expected to get to work on time by your means. Some construction jobs require workers to travel across town or across the county to reach the worksite.

What kind of work atmosphere do you find most comfortable? You may work with a crew one day, and by yourself the next. As an apprentice, you will be closely supervised during the probationary period. Throughout your training and even afterward, there are possibilities of a personality clash between you and a coworker or superior. You must solve any problems in a mature, well-behaved fashion that does not reflect poorly on your attitude or work. As in many fields of work, newcomers are often subjected to pranks from the more experienced workers.

While you are low in seniority, you will probably draw the least attractive jobs. Remember that as you gain experience and responsibility, you will be able to bid jobs that pay better and are generally easier to perform.

Are you ready to face rugged working conditions? You may work outdoors in all sorts of weather. You may also be required to carry and erect ladders and scaffolding, work at heights, dig holes or trenches, operate heavy or noisy tools and equipment, and keep a worksite tidy.

Two personal qualities that will mark you for success early in your career are a high level of self-confidence and the ability to stick with a project.

THREE LEVELS OF PREPARATION

Those looking for work as plumbing/HVAC apprentices, helpers, technicians, mechanics, and operating engineers generally represent three levels of career preparation:

- Those who have a technical education and several years of practical job experience.
- Those who are entering the field fresh from technical training and have no real work experience.
- Those seeking a job as apprentice or helper in hope of acquiring training on-the-job.

The opportunities open to each group are quite different. A quick scan of employment ads in any metropolitan Sunday newspaper will confirm that the demand is for those with a combination of training and experience. Luckily, there are still small service shops across the country where master plumbers are on the lookout for bright, ambitious young people wanting to learn a trade. The variety of apprenticeships offered in the U.S. should meet the needs of everyone looking for their first job. There are "starter-job" opportunities as well in the many specialty branches of refrigeration and air-conditioning sales, installation, and service. Your primary goal while working at entry level is to acquire a variety of job experience that will serve as a foundation for your developing career goals. You want to use the practical skills you are developing and acquire technical knowledge as well. If industry-sponsored workshops or seminars are offered, let your superior know you are interested and eager to learn. At every opportunity, demonstrate your competence in using tools and equipment as well as in communicating with coworkers and customers. Three months in a busy shop where you work with experienced mechanics and technicians in a variety of situations is more useful than a year of performing the same routine.

As for the willing but untrained, take another look at the free educational opportunities afforded by the Job Corps or military service. Even those who cannot take advantage of such training will find work, for many shops have room for the person who demonstrates youthful stamina and an eagerness to learn. Show an interest in the business and be willing to accept responsibility, and you can learn from your coworkers.

JOB-HUNTING

Finding that first job in the industry is in many ways the hardest obstacle to overcome. Yet it is the key that will open the door to your future. There are several approaches.

Graduates of trade schools may have the benefit of job placement services. Schools make a concentrated effort to establish and nurture industry contacts. If the school is doing a good job, employers will notify them when they have jobs to fill. Many schools operate cooperative learning opportunities or externships, which give them a chance to see promising students perform in real-world work situations. Many of these students find themselves with both a diploma and a job offer at graduation.

Apprentices say that their hard-earned journey-worker's card is the surest guarantee of work, particularly in the construction trades. No one gets the card without demonstrated skill and considerable experience.

APPLICATIONS AND INTERVIEWS

Aside from union hirings, the plumbing/HVAC industry relies on two standard employment tools, the job application and the personal interview. The résumé, a formal typed history of your educational and employment background, is not a requirement for job-hunting in this field. Still, you may find it helps to fill out the job application by referring to a chronological list of your experience.

At first glance, one job application seems much like the next, but individual companies have their own forms, and you should approach the task of filling them out with care. Crossed-out lines, mistakes, and erasures reflect negatively on you. It is a good idea to read the entire form before making any marks on it. Complete each item fully and truthfully, assuming that the information will be verified. If you have any questions, ask them before you begin. Sign the form if requested to do so. Also, check the back of each sheet; it may contain questions you are to answer.

Some companies do their hiring strictly through the local Job Service office, a division of the state employment bureau. Others distribute applications to job seekers who stop by. If you are applying to shops at a distance, you might inquire by phone if they are accepting applications and ask to have one mailed to you.

Typical early efforts at job-hunting include a talk with a Job Service representative and a search of the Yellow Pages or local business directories. Be sure to network, that is, let people know the kind of work you are looking for. Check with the local plumbing/HVAC supply houses. A first job as a counter person can be valuable even if you are interested in a more hands-on position later; you will make contacts in the industry and learn about parts and materials. Even social and business contacts can help you find a job. You never know: Your former teacher's brother-in-law may own the local air-conditioning repair business.

Beyond these suggestions, other resources include Civil Service job listings, private employment agencies, veterans and armed service employment agencies, and publications from the national trade associations. For example, the Refrigeration Service Engineers Society, a nonprofit educational organization, has nearly 300 local chapters. Its members hold key jobs in every branch of the refrigeration, air-conditioning sales, installation, and service field. The monthly publication it sends to members contains a classified section advertising job openings for entry-level and experienced workers. For address, see the Appendix.

THE INTERVIEW

Most hiring decisions rely heavily on the results of a job interview. That involves one or more face-to-face meetings between the job candidate (you) and someone who represents the employer. Often in a small shop, it will be the owner. Manufacturing and sales hirings may be decided by a human resources manager or an employment specialist.

It is natural to be a little nervous before a job interview, but there are ways to prepare yourself for the experience, thereby boosting your self-confidence and helping you make the best impression on the interviewer.

Start by knowing about the job you want and the company in general. If you know someone who works for the company, pick their brain for inside information. Before your interview date, stop by the office to obtain copies of company brochures or annual reports. Visit job sites to see what kind of projects they are handling. Why? You will be expected to ask some questions during the interview. These questions should show whether you want the job enough to take an interest in the company before you are hired. Your knowledge also reflects initiative, another strongly positive trait. If you sit in silence or fumble for an answer when the interviewer asks a question, you will probably lose points.

Asking questions can be difficult. You should practice them in advance so that you sound relaxed and in control of your thoughts during the interview. What topics are appropriate? You can't go wrong if you ask about:

- The job duties, working conditions, and opportunities for advancement.
- Qualifications they are looking for: physical, emotional, and educational.
- Fringe benefits that accompany the job.
- Working hours.
- Would you work alone, or in a group? How is the group organized? Whom would you report to?

- When will you know if you've been hired? What are your next steps?

Ask the questions that most interest you. These are simply suggestions. You may want to work up questions of your own.

Another way to feel more comfortable in preparing for an interview is to anticipate the questions you may be asked. Here are some typical examples:

- Why do you want to work for our company?
- Why do you think you are qualified for this job?
- Tell me about yourself and the work you like to do?
- Where do you see yourself in five years?

Later in the interview, you might be asked about your family, how you spend your spare time, what you consider to be your greatest strengths and weaknesses, and the subjects you liked best in school.

Many people find it easier to put their thoughts on paper. While you're at it, here are some additional questions to consider. What did you do on your last job? What makes you feel you are ready for this job? What are your best successes and accomplishments? What made you leave your last job? How much money do you think you should be earning? Why should we hire you instead of someone else? How long do you intend to stay with us? What would you like to tell us that is not on your application?

Of course, you won't be taking your written answers along to the interview, but don't worry. Once you have thought about the matters and formulated answers on paper, it will jog your memory should you actually be asked the question during the interview. After all, these are questions about you and your life. Who knows the answers better than you?

Practice a response to each question until you feel comfortable with it. You should strive for a genuine, sincere answer that shows something of the person you really are. All the while, remember to emphasize your strengths and admit, but downplay, any weaknesses.

THE BIG DAY

To give yourself an edge, be neat, clean, and alert. Plan to get a good night's sleep before your interview, and set the alarm to ring a little early. Wear appropriate clothes. For a construction or service shop job, a dress shirt and clean, presentable jeans or casual slacks are appropriate. If you seek a technical or inside sales position, dress up a little more, adding a tie and jacket with dress slacks. It's really difficult to overdress for a job interview. The goal is a neat, tailored look in which you are comfortable. A recent haircut is advised, and don't smoke in the reception room or during the interview, even if invited to do so.

If you have a completed application and references, make sure your name, address, and phone number appear on every page. Place the unfolded papers in a large, clean envelope or clip them securely in a folder.

Don't be late for your interview. In fact, try to arrive five to ten minutes early. Tell the receptionist your name and whom your appointment is with, then take a seat and try to appear calm. Don't shuffle through your paperwork or do anything unusual; the receptionist may have been asked to observe the behavior of job candidates.

Remember to look the interviewer in the eye, which is not to say that you should stare. Lean forward a little, and demonstrate that you are a careful listener. Don't fidget. An occasional gesture is fine; otherwise, keep your hands in your lap or on the arms of your chair. Your voice should be clear and assertive in tone. As with gestures, be conservative with your smile, but don't go through the whole interview with a poker face. Above all, don't fall into the trap (sometimes deliberately set) of complaining about past employers.

In today's economy only the largest corporations can afford full-time professional interviewers. Remember that the person you talk with may be as uncomfortable in the situation as you are.

You may be asked to take one or more tests before the interview begins. People who will be working with hand tools and machinery are often expected to demonstrate mechanical aptitudes. These trades also require proficiency in math. Increasingly, businesses want people with computer keyboard training. All can be tested in interview settings.

Remember that people who are tired or don't feel well generally do poorly on tests. Sometimes being just a little nervous actually helps to focus your attention and improves your score. Just read or listen carefully and follow the directions you are given.

In the competitive job market we all deal with today, many job-seekers face a few turndowns before scoring a success. By taking time to prepare for your interview, you will certainly improve your chances of being hired. Remember that interviewers are looking for people with initiative; workers who can recognize a problem and use their good judgment to solve it; people who understand and follow complex directions. Your preinterview work will sharpen your skills in each of these vital areas.

THE END OF THE INTERVIEW

Most interviews end with a noncommittal comment such as, "Thanks for coming in; we'll get back to you."

You may leave with no idea how you did or whether you have a chance of being hired.

Should you simply wait for a phone call that may never come? Recruitment counselors recommend that you send the interviewer a short letter of thanks within a day or two, mentioning again your interest in the job.

A week or two later, if you have heard nothing, it is permissible to make a follow-up call, asking about the status of the job. Has it been filled? Are you still being considered? If you call a few times and the response is less than encouraging, it is time to apply elsewhere. Even if you don't get the first job you go after, having been through the interview process is a valuable experience that will help you on the next go-round.

10

Opportunities for Advancement

By the turn of the century, the plumbing, heating, and cooling industry is expected to undergo a 17 percent increase in employment. This means an estimated 40,000 new jobs created by the demand for new industrial, commercial, and residential facilities for environmental and climate control. Along with new buildings and systems, job openings will result from the retirement of workers now in the field. Many union plumbers and pipefitters can take early retirement at age fifty-five. Others, union and nonunion, will move into other lines of work. This ripple effect flows down and affects all levels of job seniority. Every year opportunities open up for experienced workers to move into more challenging and rewarding tasks. Entry-level positions increase in turn, providing an opportunity for newcomers to launch their careers.

Industry leaders are aware that a shortage of technical workers will exist unless steps are taken to recruit talent into the plumbing, heating, and cooling trades. Contractors, the unions, and trade associations are working together on a recruitment effort, and to ensure that technical training is geared to the needs of a growing, changing industry. With the right combination of attitude, skills, and experience, you will be able to succeed in these trades.

Advancement may take the form of a new job title and duties, accompanied by an increase in salary and prestige. Experienced journeyworkers may become supervisors for a contractor. Office and apartment buildings, stadiums, arenas, and other large public buildings hire stationary engineers. Communities large and small hire plumbing inspectors to assure that work being done meets local standards and national performance codes. Each of these results in new job opportunities.

In addition, each year experienced plumbers and HVAC designers/technicians open their own contracting firms. One of every five plumbers is self-employed, and one in seven HVAC technicians is an entrepreneur (see Chapter 12). In turn, these former employees sponsor apprentices and hire workers of their own. In time, these people grow in skill and ability, becoming journeyworkers. Businesses grow and boost job opportunities as well.

Remembering that wage rates vary considerably across the country, it is fair to calculate a pay scale 10 to 25 percent higher for supervisors. They often receive "perks" or additional benefits such as a company vehicle to drive and from work and participation in a profit-sharing plan.

As you plan each step of your future, remember that ambition, drive, and a willingness to adapt to change lie behind successful career moves.

NEW TECHNOLOGY

Let's not forget new technology. The entire field of solar energy is experiencing important technical breakthroughs that are sure to generate new and exciting employment opportunities. Efficient, affordable solar collectors, storage systems, and distribution networks will change the nature of the heating and cooling industry in many parts of the United States. Workers who enjoy being part of innovation and working at the cutting edge of technology will reap these career rewards.

JOB MOBILITY

As has always been the case in American history, it may be necessary for people to relocate in order to benefit from the opportunities of growth and change. Several states—Nevada, Utah, North Dakota, South Dakota, and Arizona, for example—have vast stretches of undeveloped land that will attract newcomers in the decades ahead. These expanding population centers will need homes, schools, hospitals, office and shopping complexes, and government facilities. All this construction will mean jobs in plumbing, heating, and cooling. Areas of growth identified by a National Association of Home Builders survey include:

The Middle Atlantic States (New Jersey, New York, Pennsylvania)—plumbers, pipefitters, steamfitter helpers; heating, air-conditioning, and refrigeration mechanics.

East South Central States (Alabama, Kentucky, Mississippi, Tennessee)—heating, air-conditioning, and refrigeration mechanics.

East North Central States (Illinois, Indiana, Michigan, Ohio, Wisconsin)—heating, air-conditioning, and refrigeration mechanics.

West North Central States (Iowa, Kansas, Minnesota, Missouri, Nebraska, North and South Dakota)—heating, air-conditioning, and refrigeration mechanics, plumbers, pipefitters, and steamfitters.

THE LADDER OF SUCCESS

If you are interested in new challenges and opportunities, there is always a new goal to strive for. Perhaps you are already wondering what lies ahead after you achieve journeyworker status. A skilled craftworker may aspire to a number of advanced or supervisory positions, some of which will require additional training.

This is a good time to remind you how "mobile" skills are in the plumbing, heating, and cooling trades. You can advance by moving into a new segment of the industry, or by specializing in one aspect of a trade. Technological advancements in electronics, solar power, and materials applications will increase opportunities in all areas of the industry.

Advanced Jobs

Generally speaking, several job titles are used interchangeably in the fields of construction, manufacturing, installation, and maintenance/service. Briefly, they include:

Crew chief or crew leader. Position called "foreman" in the days before gender-neutral vocabularies. This man or woman directs the day's work, clarifying what is to be done and assigning jobs, if need be. Always aware of the schedule, and responsible to the next level of management, this person serves as a troubleshooter and motivates the workers. Many crew chiefs take an active role in the work to be done. Excellent communication skills are required, along with an understanding of human nature.

Job superintendent. Directs all work activities on small to medium-sized projects and specific phases of major projects. The crew chief generally reports to the superintendent.

General superintendent. This supervisor receives directions from the project manager, the job superintendent, and often the subcontractors. Communication skills are vital, both oral and written, along with the ability to follow up on details. This worker is paid to

91

assure that tasks are accomplished on time and to meet performance or quality assurance standards.

Project manager. On a large project, this person directs all construction functions, usually starting with plans and specifications. The project manager sets the work schedule and establishes procedures and job policies.

Estimator. In this job, time is not always spent at the job site. Estimators operate partly in the world of finance and partly in the repair or construction realm. To do the work, estimators need an understanding of the crucial interplay of time, labor, and money. The job is both interesting and challenging. Every company engaged in bidding contracts has at least one worker who functions as job estimator. The task may fall to an experienced supervisor or to a specialist, although in small companies it is often the owner who fills this role.

Medium-sized to large companies generally find it more efficient and profitable to have all contract costs estimated by someone who does that work only. Good estimating skills require a blend of business knowledge and practical experience, plus skill in using the tools of an estimator's trade—tables, charts, and graphs. With them, the estimator translates blueprints and specifications into materials orders, a labor force of the right size and skills, and a reasonable work schedule.

Most job estimators divide their time between desk duties in the office, site visits, and meetings with architects, engineers, and the like. During the "busy season" for a heating or cooling company, the estimator may work long hours and encounter some stress. Because controlling costs is such a vital part of the estimator's work, many companies make profit-sharing a part of the estimator's compensation package.

Expediter. Keeps jobs on schedule by reviewing and scheduling materials deliveries and workers in an expeditious manner. The expediter may also be responsible for securing necessary permits and clearances and scheduling inspections.

Plumbing/HVAC Inspector. Public health and safety are involved in these trades, making it necessary to guarantee that quality work is being performed. The drinking water resources of communities large and small must be safeguarded. In addition, a measure of consumer protection is required in regulating work. A background as a journeyworker and experience in a trade generally qualify an applicant for work as an inspector. There are various specialties in construction and repair. For instance, in some communities, plumbing inspectors are restricted to this work, whereas in others the same inspector may examine hydronic heating systems and cooling operations. The work requires knowledge of local, state, and national plumbing codes. For more about this career choice, see Chapter 12.

Maintenance and Operations

Once large buildings are erected, they need skilled people to monitor operations and schedule maintenance and repairs. Secure jobs with good pay and benefits await those who bring skills and experience in several areas of plumbing, heating, and cooling into this arena. Job opportunities exist in commercial and retail centers, sports arenas and stadiums, government buildings, power stations, apartment buildings, and the like. These jobs are identified by various titles including plant engineer and stationary engineer.

The plant engineer serves in a supervisory role to plan, assign, and supervise the work of skilled workers and semiskilled helpers who operate plumbing, heating, and cooling equipment including refrigeration and cold storage units.

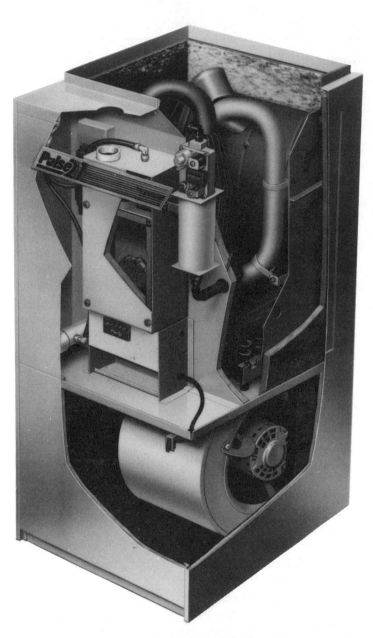

This cutaway view depicts the design of an energy-efficient pulse upflow gas furnace, typical of installations being done by today's trained HVAC mechanics and technicians (courtesy Lennox Industries, Inc.).

The work may involve stationary engines, boilers, compressors, pumps, and condensers; water, steam, and gas lines and piping; and fire protection and safety equipment. This work requires knowledge of many types of equipment and industrial safety regulations.

11

Personal Considerations

Obviously, there are plus and minus factors in every job. It's a good bet that few people are one hundred percent satisfied with their occupation at all times. The trick is knowing in advance what trade-offs you will be asked to make, then deciding how much the career means to you. Jobs in plumbing, heating, and cooling have both good points and disadvantages, all of which you would be well advised to ponder, remembering that your years of work could span half a century.

With advance planning and preparation, you can take advantage of the variety these trades offer, changing scenes and responsibilities as you choose. You will possess skills that are in demand in all parts of the country, and you should be able to make a comfortable living.

Some jobs may require travel. Sales representatives and construction workers may live away from home for days or weeks at a time. Those who work in marine refrigeration may go to sea for months at a stretch.

If you are a union member or work for a large contracting company, at times you may be assigned to a project fifty to one hundred or more miles from home. During those weeks or months you will live in motels through the workweek, perhaps with a coworker as a roommate to cut down on expenses. Some projects last six months or more, and you may decide to rent a house or an apartment, moving your family nearer the job site. Of course, if you have children of school age, this nomadic life may not be practical. If your family stays behind, the costs of separate residences, long-distance phone calls, and weekend trips home will all come out of your paycheck.

Most of these jobs offer a regular 40-hour weekday schedule, but some assignments do require shift work or weekend assignments. Emergency "callouts" are another fact of life in the business. Some of these situations will pass as you gain seniority, but you may always find your vacation plans determined by the "busy" season in your segment of the industry. A sort of Murphy's Law of heating and cooling decrees that equipment breakdowns occur when the units are in greatest demand: Air-conditioning fails in a heat wave; heating systems conk out during cold spells.

For instance, you can expect it to be too warm for comfort while you are repairing the air-conditioning. The unit may well be located on a rooftop, where the solar gain will make the air temperature even more unbearable. You may have to climb to the worksite, or face such dangers as electrical shock.

As was mentioned briefly, great physical stamina is not a requirement of the work, although you would be wise to protect your back by learning to lift and adjust loads safely. The risks of other workplace injuries are other considerations. These workers may be burned while soldering pipes, cut by power tools, or subjected to long hours of work at heights or in confined spaces.

As workers age, they may become less able or willing to tolerate the demanding working conditions. Climbing ladders, carrying heavy tools and materials, standing or kneeling in one place for a long stretch of time—the combination of these typical factors may contribute to

97

older workers' decision to move on. However, many use the skills they have acquired to develop a new career as mentioned above. Another consideration is the dirt, noise, and dust typical of worksites.

You will be expected to wear safety gear—goggles, steel-toed shoes, gloves, etc.—while performing the tasks of plumbing, heating, sheet-metal, and air-conditioning installations or repairs.

YOUTH AND WEATHER FACTORS

More than 40 percent of all construction trades workers, plumbing and HVAC workers among them, are younger than thirty. Studies show that they have a tendency to move into other fields once they reach their thirties. What jobs do they move to, and why? The answers to these questions may have a bearing on your own career direction in ten or fifteen years.

One undeniable fact about construction work is its cyclical and seasonal nature. As workers assume increased economic responsibilities, they may be unwilling to deal with seasonal layoffs. The effect of bad weather conditions is greater in construction employment than in other industries. The story is not totally one of gloom and doom, however. In many snowy regions new building methods and temporary weather shelters extend the building season. In addition, workers move into maintenance and service occupations in which seasonal layoffs are less of a problem.

Being willing to relocate is another option, since the weather is not so much a problem in the South and the West. Granted, not all workers are willing to relocate, and the trade-off of working in excessive heat is something to consider. Even in areas where construction goes on year-round, there can be downtime between the completion of one job and the start of another.

The challenge and reward of producing a tangible

product through your own efforts is becoming a rare commodity as the United States shifts to a service-based economy. Homes, high-rise buildings, and airports last for many years and stand as monuments to the skilled craftsworkers who built them. You will obviously feel a sense of pride every time you drive by a project in which you had a hand.

Also to be weighed are strong financial considerations. Plumbing and HVAC installers often earn wages double or more what comparably trained workers earn in shops and factories. Pay for service and maintenance workers is also competitive.

PERSONAL QUALIFICATIONS

While the careers we have looked at are unique in some ways, they also have certain features in common. The work requires training, experience, good judgment, and mechanical ability. It also requires manual dexterity and the ability to follow written or oral instructions.

Plumbing, heating, ventilation, and air-conditioning work requires men and women with stamina and the strength to perform active, often strenuous work. Good health, keen eyesight, physical coordination, and alertness—all these are certainly assets. Several of the jobs demand a good sense of balance and the ability to work in potentially hazardous places. Success will also depend on your respect for safety factors and the ability to take care of equipment placed in your care. Much coordination of schedules and teamwork goes on behind the scenes at a construction site, so it is important that you get along with fellow workers and supervisors.

Test Yourself

Is a blue-collar job such as those available in the plumbing/HVAC industry for you? In many ways, these jobs are appealing. You get to do interesting work with good pay and benefits, and many of the jobs offer variety and the chance to work outdoors. Still, there may be aspects of the job that you do not like. For many people who are unhappy with their work, discoveries about the "downside" of their career came *after* they had invested large sums of money or time in preparation for the job.

Before you commit to training for a career in one of these areas, carefully consider what factors hold the most appeal. Is it the physical challenge? The sense of accomplishment? Do you like being outdoors? Is it because you can work on your own for the most part?

Even after this bit of soul-searching, professional job counselors say you cannot be absolutely sure you will like a job no matter how much you learn about it in advance. Sometimes actual work experience is the only way to know for certain. Still, you can improve the odds by asking yourself some specific questions.

Let's start with the state of your health. On average, blue-collar workers are healthier than the general population, and it's a good thing, since they are often required to perform strenuous tasks.

How do you feel about doctors? Most hirings depend upon your getting a physical exam. If you are reluctant to take a physical, your chances of being hired will fade.

Do you have reliable transportation? On construction jobs at the outskirts of town, or up to fifty miles from you, you'll be expected to get to work on time. Most service jobs include the use of a lightweight pickup truck or van, but don't count on taking it to or from your residence unless you handle emergency calls.

Those employed in contract construction must save for a rainy day, since weather and project-related delays can mean days or weeks with no work. Although there will be unemployment checks and perhaps even sub pay, these don't fully replace wages.

Think about the work atmosphere in which you are most productive and comfortable. This is a male-dominated field, and although the barriers are coming down, women in nontraditional careers can still expect to earn the respect of coworkers. Don't sacrifice your dignity. Let the quality of your work and a positive attitude speak for you.

Regardless of gender, while you are the low person on the totem pole, you are likely to get the worst jobs around. This may last for months or even several years. Of course, seniority will enable you to bid jobs that pay better and are usually easier to perform. How good are you at sticking with a project when the going gets tough? How confident are you in your own abilities?

In many blue-collar occupations, rookies are subjected to a certain amount of teasing from the established workers. The young person who demonstrates a willingness to work and an even temperament will get through this phase with the least discomfort, earning the respect of fellow workers.

If You Are Still in School

What courses should you be taking in school? Math (especially algebra), earth science, computer literacy, drafting, and shop courses that teach you to use and care for tools are all useful preparation. If you have access to vocational-technical courses, you might consider blueprint reading, practical wiring, plumbing, electronic controls, and sheet-metal instruction.

Don't forget about English, speech, or communication courses, since all of these jobs require that you understand and follow directions, whether written or oral, and work well in a group.

There are several physical and emotional requirements you could work on now. Stamina, physical fitness, and a certain degree of upper-body strength are required in many of these jobs, where the pace is fast and the work strenuous. You may be required to work long hours in the hot sun.

Proven Reliability

How is your track record in school attendance? Believe it or not, it says a lot about the attitude you will display toward your job. Employers, the people who award apprenticeship slots and recruiters for the military and higher education all view a good school attendance record as a strong indication of commitment. Absent workers cost employers money, so they try to control losses by hiring people who are not likely to miss a lot of work. Likewise, training programs pack a lot of material into a day. In the interests of producing valuable employees, these slots go to the people most likely to show up and learn.

So there you have it—if you're in school, attend regularly, and pay attention, especially in those courses that lay the groundwork for your future. When you're not in school, go after work experience that will give you a clear look at the career you seek while putting you ahead of the competition for job training programs or an entry-level position.

12

Becoming Your Own Boss

Experienced workers in the fields of plumbing, heating, ventilation, and air-conditioning have great potential for making the transition from worker to boss. Whether your interest is in residential or commercial applications, or a mixture of the two, there is demand for the service you and your employees can provide. A word we hear often is *entrepreneur*, borrowed from the French and meaning someone who takes the risk of organizing and running a business in hopes of making a profit. Because they are careful problem-solvers, experienced plumbers and HVAC workers often make successful entrepreneurs.

Another route to self-employment is to become a construction or building inspector, specializing in plumbing, one of the pipe trades, heating, ventilating, air-conditioning, or refrigeration. These professionals rely on experience acquired through years of practical work experience, plus knowledge of the latest techniques to examine the construction, alteration, or repair of specific building systems. They are paid to provide quality assurance for building owners, or perhaps those who financed the construction or insure the property. But more about this specialty later. First let's examine opportunities for the self-employed contractor in construction or service/maintenance.

A BUSINESS OF YOUR OWN

If the idea of owning a business appeals to you, a wise use of the time spent acquiring on-the-job experience should also include mastering the basics of business management. Of course, that means being a worker by day and a student at night or on weekends, but a few home-study or community college courses will certainly pay off in the long run.

The key to a successful start in business is careful planning. The best time to start your own business is after you've had some experience in supervising workers and managing time and materials for someone else.

The state or community in which you intend to launch your business may have some requirements that you must meet, but these should be no real obstacle to a fully qualified journeyworker.

Most new business ventures require start-up capital, so you should have some savings or other source of funds for at least the first few months of operation. You will need to buy materials and equipment and pay for legal advice, advertising, and other services. Good financial planning is the key to protecting both your business and personal credit ratings, two essentials of a successful venture.

You will probably be called upon to make competitive bids for jobs. Understanding the interaction of time, materials, and labor requirements is essential to making a profit. From the beginning, expect to work long hours. If you don't feel comfortable handling the financial aspects, hire a reliable bookkeeper or accountant, perhaps on an as-needed basis. Financial reports, tax statements, even a payroll must be handled, all in a timely, accurate fashion.

Small business ventures are a proven source for new jobs, a fact that government recognizes and seeks to promote. You'll find sources of help and support in your community, but more about that topic later.

WHY "GO IT ALONE"?

Hard-working people make the transition from employee to employer for many reasons. The freedom to make decisions and explore opportunities is often the motivating factor. Some people go on their own because they feel it is the only way to test the full range of their talents and potential. Others frankly admit they enjoy the sense of power and control that ownership brings. The number of self-employed plumbing and HVAC workers is expected to grow as more homebuilders, general contractors, municipal governments, and other groups call upon trade specialists to perform needed work on a contract basis.

Because cash flow problems can strangle a start-up venture, you must be prepared to live on your savings account until the volume of business expands. Even if your efforts make money right from the start, you will need to buy materials and equipment and pay for expenses. Good financial planning will protect both your business and personal credit rating, another essential of a successful business.

Over and over again in interviews with the professionals who contributed to this book, we heard successful business owners stress the importance of balancing time, money, and materials. Knowing how to price your work accurately, yet competitively, is a key element in launching a business that can survive the rigors of economic change.

This situation exists because in the free-enterprise system, contractors bid competitively for the available work. In large building projects such as hospital additions, new school buildings, shopping centers, and office buildings, a general contractor is selected to perform specific elements of the work, such as erecting the building's envelope and interior spaces. Subcontractors bid to install the "systems," including plumbing, heating, ventilation, air-conditioning, and electrical wiring.

The projects are on a rather large scale, requiring detailed blueprints prepared by an architect. Complex bid documents and contracts govern the work, which may take many months to accomplish.

Service companies who deal in plumbing, heating, and air-conditioning installation, maintenance, and repair are generally organized on a smaller scale. Still, they compete for clients and need to have good management. Instead of a contract, the project is described in a simpler document known as a work order. Some service projects are bid; for other work the customer pays an hourly charge.

In the beginning, the owner of a new business keeps long hours, at the job site by day and working on bids, bookkeeping, or materials orders in the evening. Small contractors may trace their start to a single successful bid. It is important to keep a steady pace, adjusting to growth when it happens and downsizing if the economy slows. A successful contractor continues to bid jobs in a size category he or she can handle, moving up with experience as a guide.

Marketing Your Business

Most contracting firms and specialty services rise or fall on the strength of their reputation. At the job site, your employees represent you and your firm's reputation. They must understand that the future of your business depends on their attitude plus the quality of their work.

To promote the business, some contractors rent exhibit space at home shows or set up a sign with the company logo at the worksite, particularly if there is a grand opening or open house event. Display ads in telephone directories, listings in Chamber of Commerce promotional materials, or ads in the local media are other options. Still, word-of-mouth reports of the excellent work you do is the best and most cost-effective form of advertising. It helps you build a client base for repeat business and also gain valuable referrals.

PERSONNEL MANAGER

You will find yourself wearing many hats, at least in the early years of operating your business. Work in these trades can be dangerous, and you will need to be safety-oriented, as will your employees. It will be your responsibility to enforce employment laws and communicate regulations clearly to workers. You will need the ability to judge people's character in order to make hiring and firing decisions, assign jobs, and protect the good name of your business. Your ability to encourage and motivate workers will also be tested.

There is also the business office to be run. Someone must handle the phone, written communications, and bookkeeping. Tax reports and compliance documents, should you bid government contract work, will also be required.

Is it for you? Entrepreneurs generally end up working longer hours than their employees. Are you willing to invest the time and take the risks? Luckily, in the contracting business you don't have to make a lifelong commitment.

Whether you operate as a one-person venture or supervise a dozen employees, the next bit of advice will help your venture to prosper. As you take your first entrepreneurial steps, study the success of others. You will inevitably learn that "luck" has little to do with it. Experience, technical knowledge, drive, ambition, and patience, plus the ability to solve problems—those are traits that successful business owners share.

SUPPORT NETWORK

One way to increase your chances for success is to benefit from the experience of someone who has been there. A mentor is someone who has experience in your area of concern, someone who can give you good advice and teach the specialized skills of your business. SCORE, the Service Corps of Retired Executives, operates throughout the U.S. as a sort of "big brother" organization for fledging business owners.

Most state governments now offer business service centers providing programs and information of value to entrepreneurs. Local Chambers of Commerce and Industry also organize workshops to assist small business owners.

A CAREER AS INSPECTOR

Launching a business of your own in these trades need not always mean opening a sales and service shop and hiring employees. You may choose to become an inspector, or you may contract your services as a cost estimator for an architect, handling just those aspects of a building project that involve plumbing and heating/cooling systems.

The fledgling plumbing/HVAC inspector usually relies on contacts in the business for the first jobs. The task is to make an independent evaluation of structural quality and general safety of plumbing/HVAC system installations. For example, a plumbing inspector, well versed in the various building codes to be met, examines such systems as disposal, water supply, and distribution lines, plumbing fixtures and traps, vent lines, drains, and waste lines to assure that all are installed according to code and function adequately.

Increasingly, inspectors use laptop computers to carry on their work. Details such as monitoring the issuance of permits and other data can be stored and retrieved easily. Most inspections are performed visually, although measurements and various tests are also called for. Inspectors rely heavily on experience and knowledge of what constitutes a competent job. This requires a thorough background and keeping up-to-date on changes in the industry.

Inspectors are considered administrative or supervisory workers. They generally work alone, on a contract basis. This is one way to escape the physical demands of construction work, although it may still be necessary to climb ladders and work in tight quarters. In 1990 there were approximately 60,000 jobs for construction and building inspectors, a group that includes the plumbing/HVAC inspectors. Twenty-five percent worked for agencies of the federal government.

An established trend is for inspectors to become certified in their area of expertise, a process that requires additional study and training. A proficiency exam leads to the relatively new designation of Certified Building Official.

13

Vignettes

To give you a realistic look at what it is like to pursue one of the plumbing, heating, and cooling trades, this chapter is a collection of vignettes depicting a typical workday in the life of several journeyworkers, master plumbers, and certified technicians. In addition, there are glimpses into the world of those in training for careers. Some are union members, others work independently. These workers include:

- Plumbers in a kitchen and bath shop
- A construction plumber
- A building engineer
- A refrigeration mechanic
- The manager of a plumbing/heating supply firm
- A student of HVAC design
- Several business owners.

The group is drawn from a wide geographic area representing cities and towns from Boston to the Pacific Northwest. Their job experiences reflect the diversity typical of the industry, yet you will also discover that a common thread runs through their stories. These are hard-working people whose skills are in demand. Secure in their jobs and well paid for their ability and labor,

The accessible home, with design and equipment adapted for use by disabled persons, is the wave of the future as America's population ages and health care shifts to home care (courtesy Kohler).

they approach the workday with enthusiasm and have a sense of real accomplishment when a project is done.

KITCHEN AND BATH SHOP

Our first stop is at a kitchen and bath shop where the owner, a third-generation master plumber, has expanded the scope of a family business founded in 1945. It is just 8 a.m., but already Bill is on the telephone, checking on materials for a job. His wife, Terri, is working with a computer program that depicts kitchen and bath layouts and generates the plumbing layouts and a list of materials. She is responsible for keeping the materials prices updated and making sure that the showroom has up-to-date catalogs from which clients may choose fixtures, floor and wall coverings, and ceramic tile and laminated countertops. Their son is learning both sides of the business, working as an apprentice plumber and in the showroom and design office.

Ending the phone call, Bill explains, "Our goal is to provide a one-stop shopping and installation service. Clients who want a new kitchen or bath rarely want to deal with the hundreds of details and decisions that accompany the project. In the old days, a major renovation meant running all over town to see and select materials. By putting everything in one place, we make it easier for clients, and it's a great way to build business."

Of course, the shop provides customer service work, not only in single-family homes, but also at large townhouse and apartment complexes and some commercial buildings.

"Leaky faucets, clogged sinks, frozen pipes in winter—it's the same in every plumbing shop. You can't always be working on creative projects, like designing and installing a $60,000 kitchen—oh, yes, we've done some projects in that range. Usually they run closer to $20,000 with labor and materials, including the cabinets and fixtures."

Bill guides us around the showroom, with its displays of cabinet/sink units and built-ins including trash compactors, automatic dishwashers, and garbage disposals.

"Plumbers install these items, too. That's why they need some knowledge of electrical work," he adds.

In the bath department, we see jet tubs and top-of-the-line shower units with multiple sprays controlled by sophisticated electronic touch pads.

By the time we reach the design office, Terri is again

at the computer keyboard, working on a "takeoff." Such a report translates the kitchen designer's drawings into a comprehenive description of tasks to be accomplished and materials to be used to get the job done. This work provides key information on the cost of the job and the time required to accomplish it.

"The journeyworkers assigned to this project will work from two sets of documents, the blueprints and the takeoff," Bill explains. The plumbing layouts must tie in to existing lines at the house in the most direct route, for economy and efficient operation. Of course, gravity is taken into consideration, along with the requirements of the plumbing code. The transport piping covers both supply and waste lines, plus venting stacks.

"On this job, the clients want a first-floor laundry built on the other side of this wall, in a space that was once a pantry. That means running new lines and insulating them. On this job, we'll be subcontracting from a general contractor, who hires the carpenters and electrician, too. It's his job to coordinate all three phases. We just need to show up at the appointed time and keep the schedule running smoothly."

After twenty years in the business, Bill rarely picks up a pipewrench these days, unless there's a repair to be made at home or in the shop itself.

"It's mostly management that keeps me busy, and supervising the apprentices. I enjoy helping set up the displays, though. We change what's here in the shop every now and again when new products come along, and we exhibit at several home shows over the winter months.

"For years, we've kept photo albums of finished jobs that are particularly outstanding. Prospects like to see this sort of evidence of quality workmanship. In the past several years, we've done as much videotaping as taking still pictures. Kind of sweep the room with the camera panning. It's more immediate, and seems to appeal more to prospects.

"As for the hardest part of running a business, it's keeping a good, sharp crew at work. Their communication with customers is so important, but how they perform is something you just have to count on. You can't be on the job with every one of them all the time. Once a journeyworker gets a few years of experience, the really good ones want to run their own show, and who's to fault ambition? One of these days, my son will take over this business, and the journeymen can see what's down the road. They can never be top dog, so when they're in their prime, they want to strike out on their own.

"Most of our work is in the remodeling business, but about 30 percent is new construction. There's a home builder who puts up about a dozen houses a season, and when his schedule is hectic, the overload comes our way. Of course, we generally just get the labor, as it's simpler for them to order their fixtures in a package deal with all the house materials. Still, it's a part of our business that we appreciate.

"We've been gradually getting away from the heating aspects of the work, although my father did more of it in his day. We never did get into air-conditioning. Too much competition in this town. Now it's pretty much hydronics, hot-water baseboard heating systems and boilers. That's about the limit of our involvement in heating installation and repairs."

The shop operates a pair of minivans with the company logo painted on the sides and a light pickup truck. A larger van is used for transporting materials to job sites.

"The computer and fax machine are our two best electronic helpers. Aside from the showroom and design area, we have two offices; one the bookkeeper uses, the other one's mine. Then there's the pipe shop, mechanical areas, and the warehouse. Because of just-in-time inventory, we don't keep as much on hand as we did when I first started here. Part of what is now the showroom was once a parts storage area."

Bill explains that company fringe benefits include health insurance, which he terms "a major investment in our employees," and a pension fund in which the company matches employee contributions. "Of course, we have the mandatory workers' compensation, but I'm pleased to say we've had very few injuries over the years."

SERVICE AND REPAIR SHOP

Our next interview takes place in the Midwest, where a plumbing and heating business occupies a two-story corner building across the street from the fire department. The office staff and work crew have reported for the start of a busy day. A secretary is busy transcribing messages from the answering machine, aware that the shop's owner has already checked the list for emergency calls. Emergencies go to a journeyworker whose turn it is to be "on call." This duty rotates every week and, according to the supervisor, brings very little grumbling; the workers see it as an opportunity to earn overtime pay.

The telephone messages go to Don, the crew supervisor, who adds appointments as necessary to a schedule already posted on the office wall.

"A few of these calls will need to be tended to right away; the rest we'll get to later in the week," Don explains. "A lot of people joke about how hard it is to get a plumber out to their house. In this town, it's really true. We could use another journeyworker and a helper. The last time we had a job applicant walk in off the street, it was someone who had just gotten out of the Navy, and we snapped him up right away. The military turns out good, reliable workers."

Trucks and vans are rolling out of the parking area as the crew leader ticks off their missions. Two of the more experienced HVAC mechanics are scheduled for a day at a shopping plaza across town, where the company has a maintenance agreement on all heating and air-conditioning units. Their task will be to change the filters, inspect the units for worn parts or damage, and take care of any problems.

Two vans equipped with repair parts for residential and light commercial plumbing depart next. The driver of each will work alone, completing a list of work orders arranged geographically and with attention to the estimated time each job requires for completion.

"Service calls are the heart of our business," Don says."We have clients who go back ten years or more in the same house. When the dishwasher quits or a drain clogs, we get the call. You'd be surprised how many retirees in this town go down to Florida or Texas for the winter months. An important part of our work in early December is to winterize houses. Then we go back again to get everything ready when it's time for the property owner to return. We do this for nearly fifty customers."

The last vehicle to leave the loading area is a pickup truck loaded with a motorized trench-digging machine. Lengths of pipe go into the truck, along with a box of fittings, a pick, and a shovel.

"Those guys are replacing a residential waterline. The city is not responsible for leaks between its main and the property owner's interior lines. When there's a leak, it has to be fixed, or the water loss can be enormous. Not too long ago, a job like that meant some real labor. The trenching machine is a big improvement over the days when it was a pick-and-shovel job all the way."

With all the crews en route to their first assignments, Don instructs the secretary concerning some call-backs to be made, then retreats to the office where the screen of a computer terminal is glowing green.

"This is the time of day I spend checking inventories and ordering materials for upcoming jobs. We keep thousands of parts and fittings on hand, but we're sure to need things we don't have. I try to keep a close watch over this part of the business, since an inventory that's too big cuts into cash flow. Occasionally we'll need someone to 'chase parts.' Writing work orders is another time-consuming job, but it pays to do it right the first time. It takes some of the guys a while to learn that, but eventually they come around."

"In this shop, we bill on the basis of time and materials, so being able to make an accurate job estimate is not such a critical item. The shop owner does all the contract bids, and after ten years in the business, he's pretty good at it. I supervise the crew to make sure they keep to the schedule."

Continuing education has become a increasingly important part of the plumbing, heating, and cooling business. The HVAC mechanics regularly attend training sessions sponsored by manufacturers of the products they install and service. Workers view instructional videotapes to familiarize themselves with the new products with which they will be working.

A CONSTRUCTION PLUMBER

Plumbers are in demand at construction sites, and their compensation shows it. Chapter 8 on Wages and Benefits provides a comparison of construction plumbing wages and those of other blue-collar jobs. Nearly two thirds of the approximately 400,000 plumbers and pipefitters at work in the U.S. have jobs in new construction.

When we arrive in a suburban subdivision, Gregory is consulting a set of blueprints for the home, now in the final stages of construction. After introductions, he explains that the day's work is to install a spa tub and other bathroom fixtures as part of the home's master suite.

An electrician has just wired the power unit, and since the pipes are already in place, it's time for the crane to hoist the spa tub into position. The exterior bathroom wall will be built after the cumbersome tub is in place; it is a typical method for handling such a job.

This phase of the work occupies nearly an hour, after which Greg unpacks and inspects the remaining bath fixtures. A separate shower stall has been built and faced with ceramic tile. Cement board lines the walls and floor, to guard against any future water damage from a leaking pipe buried in the wall.

Two porcelain sinks are dropped into custom-made vanity tops on opposite sides of the room. The toilet, an energy-efficient water saver design, is installed in a small compartment of its own. Greg uses a set of hand tools to make connections and test for leaks, explaining each task as it proceeds.

"I've installed a thousand bathrooms by now, but probably only half as many kitchens. Can't remember the last time I worked on a new house with only one bath. Some have three or four these days. Having an electrician run wiring to the tub, now that's new, too," he adds with a grin.

Greg tells us he has had ten years of steady work with no layoffs. After a four-year apprenticeship, he received a journeyworker's card and membership in

United Association, the largest union of plumbers and pipefitters.

Holding up a narrow length of water supply line destined for one of the vanity sinks, he comments, "My older brother is a steam pipefitter who works in petroleum refineries. He'd have a good laugh at the dimensions of this pipe. He likes to see the country, and the kind of work he does suits him just fine. He's worked in Pennsylvania, New Jersey, Texas, and on the Alaska Pipeline. For the past three years he's been in Saudi Arabia with one of the big oil companies."

During the interview, we learn that plumbers install and repair the piping systems that carry water, waste, drainage, and natural gas supplies in all sorts of buildings. Construction plumbers work from blueprints, marking the location of pipes, plumbing fixtures, and appliances. They lay out pipelines in such a way as to conserve materials, but they must meet stringent inspection requirements, depending on the type of building and materials used.

"Sometimes we use plastic pipe, sometimes copper or cast iron, depending on code. Sometimes we cut holes in floors, walls, or even ceilings. When the pipes are heavy, we install steel supports to carry the weight. That's a lot of cutting, bending, and assembling the pipe, but the tools are pretty basic. To connect the pipes, you might solder, which means using a torch. Then there's the last step in a piping job, testing for leaks. We use pressure gauges. When that's done, you install the fixtures—bathtubs, shower units, sinks, and toilets. You might also install gas ranges and clothes dryers, dishwashers and water heaters."

Although other plumbers may be at work in the housing development, that doesn't necessarily mean working with them, we learn. "It's usually the carpenters and electricians who are around. You see the other plumbers driving up in the morning, or down at the union hall. When it comes to running pipes, most of the time, I work alone," Greg concludes.

BUILDING ENGINEER

The next worker has the job title Heating, Ventilation, and Air-Conditioning Specialist, with duties closely aligned with that of building engineer. He works at a large, modern office complex, which is headquarters for one of the leading insurance companies on the East Coast.

Hired in mid-1992, Derek spent a week in familiarization training, then took full responsibility for the following list of duties:

- Inspections to determine necessary repair and maintenance to prevent breakdown and major overhauls on HVAC equipment. Recommending equipment shut-downs, if necessary, for major overhauls. Planning the sequence of operations and methods for making repairs, replacements, and mechanical alterations, according to manufacturers' specifications.
- Monitoring and calibrating systems after installation; making necessary changes, adjustments, and modifications using blueprints, schematics, and manufacturers' specifications or manuals.
- Writing reports, troubleshooting HVAC equipment, checking and adjusting controls and regulators. Operating and adjusting HVAC systems as specified to maintain proper temperature and humidity. Maintaining a record of gauge readings and other operating data, noting periodic temperature and humidity readings in given areas.

To perform the work, the HVAC Specialist uses tools and air measuring devices, thermometers, manometers, and draft gauges. He must also maintain proper pH levels for all chemically treated systems, testing and treating water, using analysis kits.

The job also requires learning to operate the sophisticated Building Automation System, repairing and checking the function of equipment including absorption systems, pumps, heaters, coolers, compressors, and condensers.

Required skills include proficient use of mechanic's hand tools and the ability to read and understand blueprints.

Derek brought to the job qualifications including a high school diploma with vocational-technical certificate in building systems maintenance, plus a year of trade school courses in HVAC theory, and four years' experience as an HVAC mechanic.

"I was ready to move up, but since high school I had pictured myself running things behind the scenes at a sports arena or auditorium. Being a building engineer at one of those big complexes is still my dream—maybe the next step.

"This work is technical enough for the next couple of years. In the meantime, I plan to take some home study courses in refrigeration, maybe ice-making equipment. I supervise two people in this job, and that's a new experience. Believe me, assigning jobs to people that you know are older and have more time on the job is a big responsibility. You have to respect them, yet still get the work done. Some days there's one problem to solve after another. This building is just four years old, so there aren't too many repairs. Still, more than one hundred people work here. If something goes seriously wrong, they'd be sent home, and that would be my responsibility.

"I'm after what the job placement counselors at my tech school called 'significant experience' to improve my résumé. Someday I might even go into engineering, who knows? I'm working my way up in salary and responsibility, and it feels great."

HVAC MECHANIC

In his last job Jayson, the new building engineer, worked as an HVAC mechanic. His employer sent him to a series of training seminars offered by the manufacturer of the equipment he installed most often. Building on his tech school background, Jayson improved on such skills as blueprint reading and following manufacturer specifications. In workshop settings, he was part of a small team that learned to install refrigerant lines and piping and connect duct work and electrical power.

While hired to work on heating equipment primarily, Jayson showed a talent for ventilation and air-conditioning work that was quickly recognized by his employer.

"I learned a lot about indoor environments, and how they can affect the health and efficiency of people who work in a closed environment. Most of today's air-conditioned office buildings have windows that don't open. That makes it doubly important to pay attention to the ventilation system. People who think they have developed chronic sinus trouble or allergies may be reacting to the air quality where they work. It's something that's going to be even more important in the future. I figure it's worth learning about before everybody else has the same skills. Besides, it can be really fascinating."

The size of the equipment the HVAC worker deals with can vary dramatically, from room air conditioners to room-size units capable of cooling an office tower, Jayson explains. Industries may require really gigantic

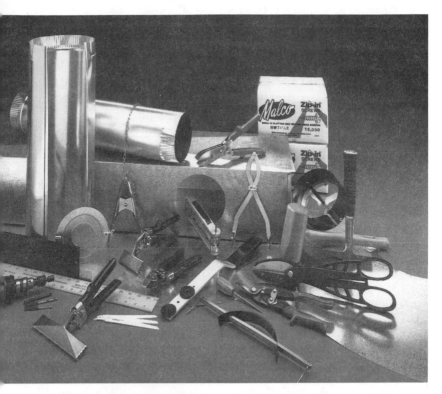

This collection of sheet-metal tools and equipment showcases the necessities of the professional's toolbox (courtesy Malco Products, Inc.).

cooling units. He cites the refrigeration units for a frozen food processing plant as an example.

"No matter what size the equipment is, they all run on the same basic principles. You'd be surprised how little installation and maintenance vary. It's certainly nothing to be afraid of, once you have the proper training and some job experience."

Jayson has also learned to enjoy working on heat pumps, which combine heating and cooling systems in a single unit. "Now you're really talking climate control," he says with obvious enthusiasm. "I love to work on an integrated system, the kind that functions according to the season and the climate control needs of the building. Usually, these mechanics specialize in one or two areas of the field, for instance, heating and cooling. If you make some good industry connections, you can go into business as an authorized dealer.

"I really enjoy installing systems. There's a lot of variety. You get to work with motors, compressors, condensing units, and evaporators. Everything needs to be installed just so, and properly balanced. It means following a designer's specifications, many times written especially for that job. Of course, there are blueprints to show where and how to do everything. You can't imagine the feeling you get, knowing you were a big part of getting something like that up and running.

"I like to read detective mysteries, and sometimes a repair job is like that. You rely on your diagnostic skills to find out what's wrong and determine where the problem might be. It's not a matter of sticking on new parts until the darned thing fires up again. We have these really sophisticated testing instruments and gauges. You need to know if the thermostats and relays are working right.

"Most of the tools we use are common enough—hammers, wrenches, metal snips, electric drills, pipe cutters and benders. I have a couple of acetylene torches, too. For air ducts and refrigeration lines, you use more specialized tools. There are voltmeters, ammeters, ohmmeters, and manometers. Don't worry. They teach you all about those in school. We use some of the same tools electricians have, especially for testing circuits and refrigeration lines."

On large, complex jobs, specialists are commonly assigned the work according to union "trade jurisdictions," a complex listing of exactly who does what in each union. For example, ductwork for a heating or ventilation contract might be crafted and installed exclusively by journeyworker sheet-metal specialists, electrical work by electricians, and piping installation by pipefitters.

REFRIGERATION TECHNICIAN

Next we meet Connie, a refrigeration technician employed by a service corporation performing contract maintenance. Customers are primarily supermarkets, restaurants, hospitals, and nursing homes within approximately fifty miles of headquarters.

"There are two regular shifts here, with an on-call shift for emergencies," Connie tells us, "since coverage is needed around the clock, seven days a week. We take care of mechanical equipment used for refrigeration and cold storage of food and other products. That means knowing the working details of refrigerating compressors, brine pumps, circulating water pumps, evaporative condensers, blowers, fans, control valves, and the other components of mechanical refrigeration systems. Some of this equipment is really big. We make repairs when they are needed, check temperatures, and regulate humidity and forced-air circulation. This is all governed by specific requirements of whatever goods are in storage—it's different for, say, frozen foods and pharmaceuticals. Many of these locations have someone keeping daily logs of temperatures, pressures, and humidity readings.

"When I started this job, I had three years' experience. It requires being able to work from plans, drawings, and mechanical or construction specifications. You have to think and act quickly in emergencies, since an equipment failure can mean losses that run into the tens of thousands, depending on the products being kept in cold storage.

125

A sheet-metal worker fabricates fiberglass ductboard using a hand-tool system known as Fasgroov. The kit features a square that eliminates the need for marking cuts or calculating add-on dimensions (courtesy Malco Products, Inc.).

"We do all the work for a chain of supermarkets, about thirty-five in all, and they've been upgrading equipment in the older markets. Installing new refrigeration cases means a lot of time spent connecting piping, fittings, and tubing. The repair work mostly involves diagnosing malfunctions, testing and charging the hermetic-type units. Sometimes I work on ammonia-based ice makers, the large industrial-size units, and brine refrigeration systems, although there's not a whole lot of that kind of work. Sometimes I supervise helpers, but most of my work is solo. I actually like that, although some people might not. The van is radio-dispatched, so even when I'm at the outer reaches of the service area, I'm still in touch with the office."

To prepare for the job, Connie earned a certificate in a technical school program that included an externship—six weeks' work "in the field," supervised by a journeyworker.

"There's another shop I pass a lot near the interstate where they do mostly repairs on refrigerated trucks, those tractor-trailer rigs they call 'reefers.' Sometimes I think about working on them, so the work would come to me and I wouldn't have so much travel, but I don't know. It's a pretty specialized branch of the business. Those guys work really hard in the summer months, and I don't know whether I'd do well with all that pressure. There are ways to get job training for that kind of work that are not too expensive, though. Some of the big equipment manufacturers have their own schools. High school kids who are just starting out would be smart to look into that aspect."

PLUMBING/HEATING SUPPLY SALES

"Anybody who wants to work in this business had better know the products," advises our next interview subject, John, who is assistant manager of a busy supply house. Well-thumbed catalogs, a microcomputer, several telephones, and product displays line the counter, behind which we glimpse aisle after aisle of shelves stacked to the ceiling with bins and boxes, some with shiny tinwork or gleaming brass contents visible.

"On any weekday morning, this is a busy place. We offer free coffee and a healthy contractor's discount, so business is brisk. Most of our customers are small shop operators and small general contractors. There are a few women plumbers in this town, and they seem to gravitate toward our store, too.

"In the past year, we've added a computerized job

estimate service, which a lot of them seem to appreciate. It saves time and makes planning a job a lot more efficient. For example, if someone is planning a boiler installation, we take the measurements and assessment of the job and in a matter of minutes can produce a materials list, with the costs itemized and even comparing different boiler sizes and efficiency ratings. It makes quick work of planning a zoned system, which is something we get lots of requests for. Lately we've been getting the requests by fax and sending them out that way, too. It saves a trip up here for contractors in neighboring towns, and most of these guys do their paperwork at night, after we close. They can put in a full day's work at the job site, knowing the paperwork will be ready and waiting when they get back to the office or home, wherever they keep the fax machine.

"That part about really knowing your merchandise means how they function and the design features. You need to demonstrate products and develop a sort of sixth sense about the ones that will sell. That means knowing your customers, the people who will buy, install, and service the products.

"If you don't think standing behind this counter is the job for you, it's interesting to realize how often manufacturers, distributors, and wholesalers in the industry hire from these supply houses. It's even more helpful if you have some field experience as a mechanic or technician. Being a manufacturer's rep can be a good job, and it could lead to even more opportunities, because the companies often send their successful salespeople on for training as sales engineers.

The next generation of heat pumps also provides most of a home's hot water needs in addition to central heat and cooling. Another technical advance makes the unit eight times quieter than earlier designs (courtesy Carrier Corporation).

"There's another aspect of this business known as outside sales. That could be a product line ranging from parts and supplies to chemicals and refrigerants. There are something like 1,500 independent refrigeration and air-conditioning supply stores in this country, not counting the distribution network of the major manufacturers.

"If you know what you're doing and have a good attitude, there's real job security in a place like this. Even when business takes a downturn, there's enough demand for repair parts and replacement work to keep us busy. Nobody lets their heating system collapse. It's a necessity. So is air-conditioning, when it comes down to it. That's about it. If you know your merchandise and you know how to treat people, you can succeed."

HVAC DESIGN
As a technical school student working toward an associate degree in HVAC Design, Brian is learning to prepare designs for heating, ventilating, and air-conditioning systems. His studies combine hands-on projects with lab assignments and theory classes in drafting, blueprint reading, computer applications, heating and cooling load calculations, and HVAC control systems.

"I'm looking at several job opportunities when I graduate in the spring. One is as an engineering assistant, another is in project management, which requires an internship first. That's to make sure I have enough background in job estimating," Brian explains.

"Within five years I'd like to be in project management. That would mean supervising a crew in design and system installations.

"I got brochures from a couple of schools and community colleges when I was a junior in high school. They offered advice that turned out to be right on target in getting ready for this training. They advised taking at least two years of algebra and one year of physics. At the time, I wondered about physics, maybe because it was a tough course for me; but now I'm glad I struggled through to the end. I took drafting, too, and that really helped with the architectural drafting I'm studying here now. It's all computer-aided, and we use the same equipment the big boys have in the real world. Technical writing was a new experience for me, but luckily, the English classes don't include poetry and literature. It's very practical in nature, unlike what you might get in a four-year college program.

"So far, the hardest thing I've encountered is my final project, designing an HVAC system from scratch. We drew numbered slips from a hat, and the numbers corresponded to projects outlined in these prepared packages. The instructor made it all a big ceremony, like we were taking on our first professional job assignments in design. They treat us as if we're working in the real world, and it sure makes you appreciate the responsibility. You get to see what things cost and how important it is to bring a project in on time without blowing the budget.

"My final project is a cooling system for a new office complex. The location is Phoenix, Arizona, and I have this huge pile of documents to govern what I do. There are architectural drawings of the finished building and everything. Sometimes when I really get into what I'm doing, I forget it's all theoretical and the project seems absolutely real.

"Right now I'm finishing up the mechanical system estimates. That means using a lot of computer-generated material on load calculations and electronic controls. You really need to understand the architectural and mechanical drawings—not just what they mean superficially, but the implications of turning those plans into a functioning reality. The next part requires laying out the cooling and heating duct systems, preparing the contractor's bid documents, and a detailed description of the project."

Variety, versatility, and a secure, promising future—from these glimpses into the lives of people at work in the plumbing, heating, and cooling industry, you can see the factors at work. If one of these descriptions sounds like the work you'd like to do, remember that such a career is within your reach. Planning and dedication will help you achieve your career goals.

14

Tomorrow's Jobs

Solving environmental problems, curbing the waste of precious natural resources, advancing space exploration, developing new tools, new products, and new techniques—all these will affect the future of plumbing, heating, and cooling.

Science is already coming to grips with the serious problem threatening the earth's ozone layer. These changes in how the cooling industry operates will affect not only how AC technicians do their work, but also how they are trained in these careers. Likewise, the need to conserve water resources has resulted in a nationwide effort to replace plumbing fixtures with new designs that use less water. Like any kind of change, these efforts have brought some disruption to the industry, but adjustments are being quickly made. The overall result will be creation of new jobs and changes in the structure of existing jobs.

For example, the Clean Air Act Amendments of 1990 strictly prohibit venting chlorofluorocarbons (CFCs) and hydrochlorofluorocarbons (HCFCs) directly into the atmosphere, because of the damage they do to the fragile protective ozone layer. It is illegal to intentionally release CFC or HCFC refrigerants into the atmosphere during the servicing, maintenance, or disposal of refrigeration or air-conditioning equipment. In addition, training

Workers on the final assembly line at Bryant Corporation's manu-facturing facility in Collierville, Tennessee, ready whole-house air conditioners for shipment (courtesy Bryant Corporation).

specifications have been enacted that require certification of all equipment reclaimers, contractors, and persons who dispose of such items. Service technicians are required to maximize recycling efforts, according to the Environmental Protection Agency (EPA), the branch of the federal government responsible for overseeing the rules.

A complete phase-out of CFCs is targeted for January 1, 1996, by which time owners of any equipment that does not meet EPA requirements must convert or replace it with equipment that uses alternative refrigerants.

This phasing-out plan is a global effort. The U.S. was one of twenty-three countries that agreed to limit use and production of CFCs, an action taken in 1987 and known as the Montreal Protocol on Substances that Deplete the Ozone Layer. No doubt you will learn more about the historical perspectives in your career training.

The Montreal Protocol initially required a 50 percent reduction in CFC production worldwide by the year 2000. Since the Montreal conference, scientists have discovered even greater damage to the ozone layer, prompting a speeding up of the phase-out deadline. Petroleum resources will also affect the industry, determining how various appliances and equipment are designed, manufactured, installed, and serviced. An even more profound impact will be made by advances in solar energy technology, a relatively new field that is worth a closer look.

SOLAR-POWERED CAREERS

The sun is a tremendous source of energy not only for heating air and water, but also for conversion to electricity. This "free" power source has almost limitless residential, commercial, and industrial applications. The key is in harnessing the power in cost-effective ways.

135

A number of job opportunities already exist connected to renewable energy and the energy conservation industries. These jobs range from research and development to manufacturing and distribution processes. There will be work for engineers, managers, technicians, sales and marketing experts, information specialists, and skilled and unskilled laborers.

Energy conservation specialists will also find work in the related fields of finance, investment, real estate, insurance, and law. Those who design, build, or install solar heating or hot water systems, who put energy conservation measures into effect, or who advise on such projects will enjoy the greatest career growth.

For insight into the four primary types of work that will develop, consider these four emerging careers defined by the U.S. Department of Energy:

Energy-Conscious Designers, who use their knowledge of architecture, the building trades, solar components, engineering, energy conservation, and renewable energy options to design solar and energy-conserving buildings and systems.

Energy-Conscious Designer/Builders, who use their knowledge of architecture, the building trades, and energy conservation measures to construct solar and energy-conserving buildings and additions.

Solar and Conservation Installers, who combine the skills of roofing, plumbing, sheet-metal work, electrical work, insulating, masonry, and carpentry to install active solar heating and hot water systems in buildings and increase building energy efficiency.

Energy Conservation Consultants, who advise on all aspects of active or passive solar systems, energy conservation measures, and renewable energy options, including design, financing, economic feasibility, and sizing. Energy auditors analyze energy consumption and sources of heat loss in homes and other structures. Energy service companies examine energy consumption patterns and needs in commercial and industrial buildings, suggesting conservation plans.

RELATED TECHNOLOGY FIELDS

New careers are also on the horizon in such renewable energy technologies as wind power, geothermal energy, hydroelectric power, ocean energy, and bioconversion. Large-scale solar technologies include opportunities such as solar thermal power generation. Of course, such jobs will be concentrated in geographic areas where the amount and type of solar radiation is greatest. Primarily, the jobs will focus on the desert Southwest.

The biomass and alcohol fuels industries will generate employment opportunities linked to agriculture and forestry, chemical processing, sales, and marketing. Specializing in small-scale, rural, or appropriate technology applications may lead to a career with overseas employment opportunities.

Information on tomorrow's jobs in plumbing, heating, and cooling will become available to the new generation of workers through colleges, technical schools, community groups, government agencies, the news media, trade unions, and trade associations.

Interested in reading more about solar careers? Ask your librarian for information about such publications as *Solar Age, Renewable Energy News*, or *Solar Engineering and Contracting*.

PLANNING YOUR FUTURE

Are you concerned how your career education will mesh with these changes in the industry? Don't be. Work in the renewable energy field is not necessarily a new career so much as a specialization within an existing one. For example, a person trained as an HVAC technician may evolve into a contractor specializing in active solar heating installations. Continuing education and hands-on experience with the new products and techniques will be available when you are ready to begin specializing. The industry is actively working on programs to help in this career evolution. The National Association of Plumbing, Heating and Cooling Contractors is cooperating with the U.S. Department of Energy and other agencies in planning an efficient transition, a process that has already begun.

The years ahead promise to be exciting ones for people with mechanical skills, technical education, and a winning attitude. The sky, or perhaps in keeping with our discussion of solar energy, we should say the sun, is the only limit.

15

Career Advice from Industry Insiders

The National Association of Plumbing, Heating and Cooling Contractors has a vested interest in your career decision. This trade association represents plumbing/HVAC businesses across the nation, and its members are vitally concerned about the upcoming generation of craftworkers. It is from those ranks that they will hire new workers to handle increased business and replace retirees.

To help resolve career decisions, the PHC Contractors have developed the following information, presented in a question-and-answer format for easy reference.

Should I Learn a Skilled Trade?

Yes, if you have the natural ability to work with your hands as well as your mind. In terms of pay, steady work, and being happy at a job, the worker with a skill has the advantage over the one without a skill. Having a skilled trade, whether or not you stick to it throughout life, often means the difference between confidence and uncertainty, self-reliance and dependency. The unskilled person is easily replaced. Lower earnings and less job satisfaction reflect the unskilled status.

What Skill Should It Be?

Plumbing-heating-cooling work requires a combination of mechanical aptitude and the ability to solve engineering problems by careful thought and creativeness. There is enough variety in industry jobs to satisfy almost anyone. If you have intelligence and a desire to build things, you are almost sure to find the plumbing-heating-cooling industry a source of satisfaction and success.

Are There Good Job Opportunities?

If you are ambitious and apply yourself, you will be welcomed into the industry. Once well trained and highly skilled, you will be in demand.

For a number of years, plumbing and related pipe work has been increasing in importance in many types of building construction. Future advancement is encouraged by active development of new products and techniques initiated by joint efforts of the industry.

How Long Will It Take Me to Earn a Good Income, and What Are My Chances of Advancement?

It takes about four years to reach journeyworker status, that is, to be able to take the full responsibility of a skilled craftsman. Chances for advancement in the industry are determined, of course, by the growth of the industry, the contractor you work for, and your own intelligence, skill, and ambition.

All foremen and most superintendents in the industry have come up through the ranks. If you apply yourself, you have a good opportunity to move into one of these spots at some time in your career. Or, characteristic of the industry, you can move into estimating, sales, design, or a management job in the office. You may perhaps go into business for yourself.

Are the Working Conditions Safe?

Since enactment of the Occupational Safety and Health Act of 1970, prevention of accidents has taken top priority in general construction. The plumbing-heating-cooling industry has expended vast amounts of time, money, and effort in training employees in safety and health techniques. The industry is concerned about worker safety and productivity. Logically, an employee whose health and safety are assured on the job is sure to be more productive.

Can I Become an Employer Myself?

The plumbing-heating-cooling industry is composed of many small shops, as well as larger ones, owned and operated by men and women who came up from the ranks through apprenticeship. In many states and municipalities, it is necessary for a journeyworker plumber to pass a master plumber examination before entering the business as a contractor. After you have worked as a journeyworker, you will have a solid background for the master's examination.

What If I Change My Mind?

Almost everyone who enters the plumbing-heating-cooling industry stays with it. Those who leave go into maintenance or other phases of the construction industry or into the manufacturing side of the trade. There is always considerable demand by manufacturers and wholesale distributors for employees with a good technical background.

What Special Abilities Should I Have?

Plumbing-heating-cooling is somewhat of a custom industry. No two jobs are exactly alike, and employees must have good judgment. Good judgment means both intelligence and the ability to adapt oneself to new or unusual situations as they occur. The industry needs workers who have the ability to master physical science and who are skillful with their hands. Plumbing and pipefitting is creative work. When you have become a skilled craftsworker and are handed a set of architectural drawings, you must be able to lay out the job and determine that it will perform the best service and conform to state and municipal ordinances.

Physical requirements include average strength and coordination and general good health. The work keeps you outdoors a large part of the time, and occasionally it is necessary to work under awkward and uncomfortable conditions.

Is It a Progressive Industry?

An industry that pays high wages and whose existence is necessary to the maintenance of public health must continually develop new ideas and methods. Plumbing-heating-cooling may not seem to have the romance and glamour of other industries, but no industry is more conscious of the need for improvement and expansion of its service. Consider the tremendous advances during the past twenty-five years in the design of plumbing fixtures. Consider the fact that plumbing—and thus good sanitation—is now taken as a matter of course, whereas only a few years ago it was a luxury. Consider also the tremendous advances in automatic heating, air-conditioning, automatic temperature controls, and development of new, lighter materials for easier installation. These are ample proof of a progressive industry.

How Do I Get Started?

If you are presently enrolled in high school, it is recommended that you complete your high school education. You may find it helpful to emphasize certain courses of study in your junior and senior years: algebra, plane geometry, chemistry, and of course, English and speech.

Ask local plumbing-heating-cooling contractors for more detailed information about the trade in your location. Talk with as many people in the trade as possible. The more information you have, the better equipped you will be to form realistic plans for your career. Plumbing-heating-cooling contractors are listed in the Yellow Pages. You may also obtain more information from your high school guidance department or the state Department of Labor.

What Will I Learn in Apprenticeship School?

During your apprenticeship, besides on-the-job training, you will spend part of your time in the classroom. Subjects you will study are: mathematics applicable to pipe work; physics with emphasis on liquids and gases; elements of hydraulics and heat; mechanical drawing; and plumbing theory. Theory instruction includes materials, sanitation, elements of bacteriology, and piping systems.

Glossary

apprentice Person, usually between eighteen and twenty-four years of age, who is learning a trade through a combination of on-the-job training and classroom instruction.

agreement, collective bargaining Contract negotiated between a union and an employer to cover workers' wages, hours, fringe benefits, and working conditions.

blueprint Reproduction by a photographic process of an architect's or designer's construction drawing.

building trades Skilled trades in the construction industry, including bricklayers, carpenters, electricians, masons, painters, and plumbers.

compensation The package of wages and benefits, both current and deferred (as with vacation time or retirement pensions), that workers receive in exchange for their work.

contractor Person or company who agrees to do a specific job under conditions and prices spelled out in a legal agreement called a contract.

craftsperson Artisan whose work or occupation requires particular training and practice.

estimator Worker who calculates the amount of materials, labor, and general costs required to accomplish a job.

foreperson Leader of a work crew, usually specially trained or experienced.

fringe benefits Benefits over and above the basic wage rate; for example, health insurance, paid vacation days.

inspector Person who examines a project or work

144

element to guarantee that standards of safety or quality are being met.

journeyperson Worker who has completed apprenticeship training.

layoff Interruption in employment usually related to a construction slowdown or inclement weather.

layout work Reading blueprints and specifications and translating that information into specific instructions for workers.

modular Involving precision or standardized parts made for fast and efficient assembly on-site.

on-the-job training Paid employment that combines work with learning; often combined with classroom instruction in apprenticeship programs.

overtime Time spent on the job that exceeds the basic workday or workweek as defined by law. Premium rates of pay apply to such hours.

subcontractor Person or company that agrees to perform certain skilled work on a building being erected by a general contractor. Typical subcontract specialties are in electrical wiring, plumbing, and heating.

superintendent Supervisor who directs the work of forepersons and their crews at a construction site.

takeoff Process of compiling a materials and/or cost list from the architectural drawing of a plumbing or heating project; usually used in the context, "to do a takeoff."

troubleshoot The process of testing and/or diagnosing malfunctions in electrical circuits, appliances, machinery, or other equipment.

Appendix

Unions, Trade Associations, and Industry Publications

Journals published by plumbing, heating, and cooling trade associations and the associations themselves provide a good way to keep your finger on the pulse of the industry while you are preparing for your career. Labor unions in these crafts have information regarding apprenticeship programs and membership benefits. Trade associations often sponsor student memberships, offering access to internships, conventions and conferences, employment opportunities, and other benefits.

Remember that organizations and publications move occasionally. If you find an address is no longer current, consult a telephone directory or directory of associations or publications at the library.

Unions and Associations

American Society of Plumbing Engineers
210 Thousand Oaks Boulevard
Westlake, CA 01362

Conservation and Renewable Energy Inquiry and Referral Service (CAREIRS)
P.O. Box 8900
Silver Spring, MD 20907

National Association of Plumbing, Heating and Cooling Contractors
P.O. Box 6808
Falls Church, VA 22046

Plumbing, Heating and Cooling Information
Bureau
303 East Wacker Drive
Chicago, IL 60601

Refrigeration Service Engineers Society
1800 Oakton
Des Plaines, IL 60018

Sheet Metal Workers' International Association
1750 New York Avenue NW
Washington, DC 20006

Solar Energy Industries Association
777 North Capitol Street NE
Washington, DC 20002-4226

United Association of Journeymen and Apprentices
of the Plumbing and Pipefitting Industry of the
U.S. and Canada
901 Massachusetts Avenue NW
Washington, DC 20001

TRADE JOURNALS AND PUBLICATIONS

Because of their specialized audience, you will rarely
find the following magazines on newsstands. They carry
reports of new products making an impact in plumbing,
heating and cooling, along with technical articles, book
reviews, convention news, and announcements of valuable training programs. Many publish classified and
display help-wanted and position-wanted ads.

Air Conditioning, Heating and Refrigeration News
(weekly)
P.O. Box 6000
Birmingham, MI 48012

Articles cover technical, training, and business subjects. Annual directory lists every manufacturer, distributor, wholesaler, exporter, and association in the industry, along with product listings and industry statistics.

Air Conditioning and Refrigeration Business (monthly)
614 Superior Avenue West
Cleveland, OH 44113

Articles cover merchandising, engineering, installation, and maintenance of various types of components, equipment, tools, and instruments.

ASHRAE Journal (monthly)
ASHRAE Association
345 East 47th Street
New York, NY 10017

Articles cover technical applications of AC and ventilating systems, heating and refrigerating systems, and components.

Contractor Magazine (biweekly)
Berkshire Common
Pittsfield, MA 01202

Articles emphasize management issues such as merchandising, technical subjects, features, and news items in the field of plumbing, heating, cooling, and piping.

Reeves Journal
2048 Cotner Avenue
Los Angeles, CA 90025

Articles and news items are aimed at smaller contractors in plumbing, heating, and air-conditioning.

RSC/Refrigeration Service and Contracting
1800 Oakton
Des Plaines, IL 60018

Official publication of Refrigeration Service Engineers Society, which offers three-year technical courses in the industry.

SNIPS (monthly)
1949 North Cornell Avenue
Melrose Park, IL 60160

Articles and news items directed to contractors in sheet-metal, warm-air heating, ventilation, and air-conditioning work. Reviews new products, catalogs, literature, and trade association activities. The editors also maintain a publication distribution program that lists nearly every book and other publication available on the topics. Single copies of the catalog are free.

Solar Heating and Cooling (bimonthly)
20 Community Place
Morristown, NJ 07960

Articles on the practical design and application of solar systems, including new products.

Solar Industry Journal (quarterly)
Solar Energy Industries Association
777 North Capitol Street, NE
Washington, DC 20002-4226

The Wholesaler (monthly)
110 North York Road
Elmhurst, IL 60126

Tabloid magazine with emphasis on news of the plumbing, heating, and air-conditioning industry; features on the profitable management of a wholesale firm and its relations with dealers and contractors.

For Further Reading

Alerich, Walter N. *Electricity Three: Motors and Generators, Controls and Transformers*, 4th ed. Albany, NY: Delmar Publishers, 1986.

Almond, Joseph. *Plumber's Handbook*, 8th ed. New York: Macmillan, 1991.

Apprenticeship: Past and Present (free). Bureau of Apprenticeship and Training Administration, U.S. Department of Labor, 200 Constitution Avenue NW, Washington, DC 20210

Brumbaugh, James E. *Heating, Ventilating and Air Conditioning Library* (3 vol.). New York: Macmillan, 1984.

Careers in the Crafts (single copy free). International Association of Machinists and Aerospace Workers, 1300 Connecticut Avenue NW, Washington, DC 20036.

Gilbertson, Thomas A. *The HVAC Design Manual.* Englewood Cliffs: Prentice-Hall, 1992.

Goetsch, David L. et al. *Mathematics for the Heating, Ventilating and Cooling Trades.* Englewood Cliffs: Prentice-Hall, 1988.

Harris, Cyril M. *Practical Plumbing Engineering.* New York: McGraw-Hill, 1991.

Havrella, Raymond. *Heating, Ventilating and Air Conditioning Fundamentals.* New York: McGraw-Hill, 1981.

Hedden, Jay. *Heating, Cooling and Ventilation: Solar and Conventional Solutions*. New York: McGraw-Hill, 1991.

Hicks, Tyler G. *Plumbing Design and Installation Reference Guide*. New York: McGraw-Hill, 1986.

Hornung, William J. *Plumber's and Pipefitter's Handbook*. Englewood Cliffs: Prentice-Hall, 1984.

Lytle, Elizabeth Stewart. *Careers in the Construction Trades*. New York: Rosen Publishing Group, 1992.

McConnell, Charles N. *Plumber's and Pipefitter's Library* (3 vol.). New York: Macmillan, 1989.

Meltzer, M. *Passive and Active Solar Heating Technology*. Old Tappan, NJ: Prentice-Hall, 1985.

Neufeld, Rose. *Exploring Nontraditional Jobs for Women*. New York: Rosen Publishing Group, 1989.

Ricci, Larry. *High-Paying Blue-Collar Jobs for Women: A Comprehensive Guide*. New York: Ballantine Books, 1981.

Shertzer, Bruce E. *Career Planning: Freedom to Choose*, 3d ed. Boston: Houghton-Mifflin, 1990.

Spence, William P. *Construction: Industry & Careers*. Englewood Cliffs: Prentice-Hall, 1990.

Starr, William. *Electric Wiring and Design: A Practical Approach*. Englewood Cliffs: Prentice-Hall, 1983.

Sumichrast, Michael. *Opportunities in Building Construction Trades*. Lincolnwood, IL: National Textbook Company, 1985.

Traister, John E. *Vest Pocket Guide to HVAC Electricity*. Englewood Cliffs: Prentice-Hall, 1989.

————. *Heating, Ventilating and AC Design for Building Construction*. Englewood Cliffs: Prentice-Hall, 1987.

Index

U
UA, *see* United Association
union, 33–37, 42, 74, 88
    jurisdiction, 12–13, 124–125
    membership, 26, 96
United Association of Journeymen
    and Apprentices, 34, 35

V
ventilation, 2, 14–16
vent system, 50

W
wages, 8, 18, 71–77, 89, 99
waste system, 50, 119

water, potable, 50, 93, 119
water treatment equipment, 26
Wider Opportunity for Women
    (WOW), 61–62
Women in the Building Trades, 61
Women in the Skilled Trades
    (WIST), 63
women, opportunities for, 58–70,
    101
working conditions, 33, 79
work order, 39, 48, 106, 117

Y
YMCA (Young Women's Christian
    Association), 59, 61